Analytics for Leaders

Analytics for Leaders provides a concise, readable account of a complete system of performance measurement for an enterprise. Based on over twenty years of research and development, the system is designed to provide people at all levels with the quantitative information they need to do their jobs: board members to exercise due diligence about all facets of the business, leaders to decide where to focus attention next, and people to carry out their work well. For senior officers, chapter openers provide quick overviews about the overall approach to a particular stakeholder group and how to connect overall performance measures to business impact. For MBA students, extensive supporting notes and references provide in-depth understanding. For researchers and practitioners, a generic statistical approach is described to encourage new ways of tackling performance measurement issues. The book is relevant to all types of enterprise, large or small, public or private, academic or governmental.

Additional resources including downloadable articles are available at www.valuemetrics.com.au.

NICK FISHER is the founder of ValueMetrics Australia, an enterprise that carries out research and consulting primarily in the area of Performance Measurement. Dr. Fisher carries out R&D projects around the world, with particular emphasis on improving quantitative reports to boards and top management. His more recent work has focused on measuring Research Quality and measurement of public policy. He is also a Visiting Professor of Statistics at the University of Sydney.

Analytics for Leaders

A Performance Measurement System for Business Success

N. I. FISHER
University of Sydney and
ValueMetrics Australia

CAMBRIDGE
UNIVERSITY PRESS

University Printing House, Cambridge CB2 8BS, United Kingdom

Published in the United States of America by Cambridge University Press, New York

Cambridge University Press is part of the University of Cambridge.

It furthers the University's mission by disseminating knowledge in the pursuit of education, learning and research at the highest international levels of excellence.

www.cambridge.org
Information on this title: www.cambridge.org/9781107045569

First published 2013

Printed in the United Kingdom by Clays, St Ives plc

A catalog record for this publication is available from the British Library

Library of Congress Cataloging in Publication data
Fisher, N. I.
Analytics for leaders : a performance measurement system for business success /
N.I. Fisher.
    pages   cm
ISBN 978-1-107-04556-9 (Hardback)
1. Management–Statistical methods.   2. Business planning–Statistical
methods.   3. Performance.   4. Organizational effectiveness.   I. Title.
HD30.215.F58 2013
658.4′013–dc23   2013018718

ISBN 978-1-107-04556-9 Hardback

Additional resources at www.valuemetrics.com.au

To Homer Sarasohn and Myron Tribus
Wise men whose work transformed countries, industries and cultures

Generous and steadfast friends

Homer Sarasohn, 2001. Photograph: Lisa Sarasohn

Myron Tribus, 2001. Photograph: Michael King

Contents

Exhibits

Preface

Day after day, day after day,
We stuck, nor breath nor motion;
As idle as a painted ship
Upon a painted ocean.

"The Rime of the Ancient Mariner" – Samuel Taylor Coleridge

THE NEED FOR ANALYTICS

Is that how your enterprise is going – or rather, not going? Which lever should you pull to give it the best impetus? Why this lever and not another lever? *How will you decide? And how will you know whether you've changed things in the way you intended?*

The purpose of this book is to describe how to obtain performance measures that will provide you with a sound basis for answering these questions: measures that can help you focus your efforts on improvements likely to have the biggest impact on your most pressing business issues – how to increase market share, how to reduce staff turnover, how to work better with suppliers, how to build community support for a development.

Most leaders now recognize that it isn't good enough to rely simply on some financial measures supported by a few indicators such as market share. More information is needed if companies – let alone, countries – are to guard against the sorts of risks that resulted in the 2007–2008 Global Financial Crisis. And there are numerous other risks that can also cause the downfall of the most well-intentioned leader who hasn't got timely and actionable data.

If you're on the Board of Directors, you are indeed *obligated* to exercise due diligence with the whole spectrum of risks confronting your enterprise in order to assure good corporate governance.[1]

The other side of this coin is that by harnessing the power inherent in systematic gathering and analysis of appropriate performance data, you can make a critical difference to the competitive position of your enterprise. Recent books by Thomas Davenport and co-workers[2] are full of examples showing how enterprises are increasingly turning to the use of data and associated *business analytics* to achieve greatly enhanced performance. In the words of Davenport and Harris:[3]

> By analytics, we mean the extensive use of data, statistical and quantitative analysis, explanatory and predictive models, and fact-based management to drive decisions and actions.

And, in a discussion about practicing "Big-Picture Thinking," they comment:

> High-potential targets for business analytics vary by industry dynamics and, of course, by how firms add value in the marketplace.[4]

This provides a natural launching platform for our discussion.

FOCUS ON STAKEHOLDER VALUE

Our starting point will be to define and measure the *Value* that your enterprise delivers to your stakeholders; that is, to each of the groups whose support you need to survive and thrive.

Regardless of your line of business, you need to keep the owners happy with their investment. And then there are the people you'd like to have as customers; the people you'd like to employ; the key partnerships and suppliers you need to run your business; and, finally, the wider community, whose sanction for a proposed course of action may make or break your company.

In other words, we start by describing and measuring *outcomes for stakeholders*.

However, these outcomes resulted from actions you took in the past. What you really need is a set of lead indicators that tell you where the enterprise is actually heading.

The *measurement system* we describe seeks to align the people and processes in your enterprise with the goal of delivering superior Value to all your key stakeholder groups. It does this by separating the system into two basic components:

1. a performance measurement *framework*, that defines the sorts of measures that are needed at each level of the enterprise, to help people do their jobs well; and
2. a process for *managing stakeholder value*, that helps you put these measures in place and use them to best effect.

Of course, like any model for what happens in an enterprise, this model for a performance measurement system is a considerable over-simplification of reality. Nonetheless, it may help guide our thinking in a usefully structured way. As the eminent statistical scientist George Box famously observed:

> All models are wrong but some are useful.

Davenport and co-workers, in discussing how to overcome "sticking points" to embedding analytics in business processes, suggest that the key to this is

> to get data assets well organized into a robust representation of the business.[5]

We contend that the process of managing stakeholder value described in the following pages provides a natural organizing principle for this purpose. From a different perspective, it is also a natural generalization of Richard Normann's observation that[6]

> the logic of value production in society and in service industries is changing at a rapid rate.

Sutcliff and Donnellan noted that[7]

> High performance businesses have a very strong value orientation. They firmly ground their strategy in driving value and the key

result measures of performance are linked to total returns to shareholders. They clearly understand their value drivers and have a proven process for identification and prioritization of the key causal drivers. They focus on the few critical drivers of value and causal information necessary and sufficient for managing their business.

The material in this book is very much in this spirit. The overall system is described in three basic steps:

1. Stakeholder analysis: who are the main groups and sub-groups of stakeholders for an enterprise?
2. What are the different types of metrics that are needed, at different levels of the enterprise, from the Board to the shop floor, to help people do their jobs?
3. How can you go about identifying the particular metrics needed for your enterprise?

HOW TO READ THIS BOOK

The book is designed to be read in different ways, as shown in Exhibit 0.1:

EXHIBIT 0.1. How to read this book. Depending on your purpose, you can get an overview of the system, or gain a fuller understanding of how to do it, or go into the operational aspects.

Purpose	What to read
1. To understand what it's about	Chapters 1–4
	Part I of each of Chapters 5–8
	Chapters 9 and 10
	Appendix: Don't be fooled by statistics
2. To understand how to do it	Chapters 1–10
	Appendix: Don't be fooled by statistics
3. To understand the operational aspects	Chapters 1–14
	Appendix: Don't be fooled by statistics

The first ten chapters describe the system: what it is, how it works, and examples of its use. If you simply want an overview, just read Part I of each chapter when you get to Chapters 5–8, which are particularly relevant to leaders interested in the benefits to be gained from a properly designed performance measurement system.

Chapters 10–14 look at how to start implementing the performance measurement system in your enterprise. They are particularly relevant to the person who is told to "Make it happen" and who needs to appreciate the practical aspects in some operational detail.

USE OF CASE STUDIES

Case studies have been selected to illustrate different aspects of the methods presented. For example, a case study relating to managing Customer Value focuses specifically on the critical issue of finding good operational internal metrics. On the other hand, a case study on managing People Value illustrates the power of continuously acquiring stakeholder data in terms of enabling timely decisions.

OTHER APPROACHES TO PERFORMANCE MEASUREMENT

The topic of performance measurement[8] has received some attention in the management literature, without generating the range of competing approaches that one might have expected. There are many more articles warning about the hazards of poor performance metrics than articles recommending approaches to avoid peril.[9]

The simplest approach is to look for a very small set of generic metrics that can be used throughout an organization or, equivalently, at all scales of measurement from micro to macro. Fisher and Nair observe that[10]

> The power of this concept is that it could be used to focus
> communication at all levels of the organisation: in the words used
> by a senior industry figure to one of the authors, "I want to be able
> to drill down through management layers with a single metric, to
> find out what's causing a problem"

and discuss two examples: the Motorola metrics of cycle time and "Six Sigma"; and Eliyahu Goldratt's advocacy of three key performance measurements: throughput, inventory and operating expense.[11] However, Fisher and Nair conclude from their discussion that

> the search for a single generic measure is almost certainly going to be fruitless; and once more measures are included, the whole rationale of the approach is lost.

Neely and co-workers[12] provided a brief overview of performance measurement *frameworks* developed over the last quarter-century. The most popular proposal has been due to Robert Kaplan and David Norton, in a stream of publications relating to the Balanced Scorecard.[13] As originally described, their approach defines four *perspectives* – Customer, Internal, Innovation and Learning, and Shareholder[14] – and posits "a set of measures that gives top managers a fast but comprehensive view of the business. The balanced scorecard includes financial measures that tell the results of actions already taken. And it complements the financial measures with operational measures...that are the drivers of future financial performance."

The *system* described in this book accommodates the Customer and the Shareholder (or more generally, the Owner) perspectives directly, and adds the perspectives of three other critical stakeholder groups, while treating the operational aspects in another part of the system. Atkinson and co-workers, in discussing a similar stakeholder approach to strategic performance measurement, commented on the "incomplete" nature of the Balanced Scorecard as a basis for a performance measurement system.[15,16]

Put another way, our summary reports for enterprise leadership are comprehensive in terms of coverage of stakeholder interests, and are confined largely to strategic and tactical metrics. Generally speaking, it is not the responsibility of top management to be monitoring operational measures, unless they are mission-critical.

There are other published models[17] that address aspects of a performance measurement system, but without capturing the full intent of the two components – a Performance Measurement Framework and a process to populate the Framework with metrics and use them to best effect.

As recently as 2007 there was still debate in the literature about the definition of a business performance measurement system.[18] For our purposes, it's simple: it is a system that provides the people in an enterprise with the quantitative information that they need to do their jobs well.

WHAT THIS BOOK IS AND IS NOT

This is *not* a book on how to be an effective leader. Leaders need the knowledge and information we describe, but the book is not about leadership skills, methods, approaches, and so on.

We do *not* get into the world of designing complex databases and information systems. However, the system we describe does call into question the content of large multi-national corporate IT systems. It implies that data need to be arranged into a logical cause-and-effect hierarchy, and so has implications for the design of databases. It can serve as a checklist to evaluate your current information systems.

The book is concerned with how to identify, obtain and present appropriate quantitative information to inform decision-making, an essential requirement if leaders are to be effective.

We are talking about creating Value for everyone, which we see as the purpose of an enterprise. But what you cannot measure, you cannot create and then manage. We describe what you have to measure to create and manage Value. In fact, we go further: we claim that only the best Value wins in each of the markets you compete in. We show how to measure and track *competitive* Value.

Finally, we show how all Value is judged between what one gets versus what one gives, and how that can be broken down into very understandable, measurable and manageable levers and sub-levers. This means that the leadership team can make sound decisions about where to spend the scarce time, energy, money and resources of the enterprise.

INTENDED READERSHIP

We believe that this book will be of interest – and value! – to a number of audiences.

Firstly, we trust that leaders will find it helpful in understanding what information they need to see regularly, to help their enterprise navigate an increasingly competitive environment with an increasing requirement to manage a wide range of risks.

Next, we have sought to provide guidance to people charged by their leadership with implementing performance measurement in their enterprise.

Another important audience relates to research, teaching and learning:

- Methodological aspects will be of interest to academics and practitioners in areas such as Business Administration, Management, Marketing, Human Resources (HR), Statistics, Environmental Monitoring, and Science Communication.
- Experience has shown that the material is well suited to workshops and executive education programs of the sort run by business schools.

The basic approach to adopting the Performance Measurement Framework has been trialed extensively and successfully with owners and managers of small and medium enterprises (SMEs).

NOTES

1 Although sets of Corporate Governance principles vary from country to country in their emphasis on shareholder interests vis-à-vis those of other stakeholders (typically, they talk about "respecting the rights" of shareholders compared with "recognizing the legitimate interests" of other stakeholders), they generally include mention of all types of stakeholder. This implies a full spectrum of risks to be managed.

2 Davenport and Harris (2007), Davenport *et al.* (2010).

3 Davenport and Harris (2007), page 7.

4 Davenport *et al.* (2010), page 77.

5 *Ibid*, page 133.

6 Normann (2001), page 19; earlier (page 11), Normann observes that: "value creation in today's economy is increasingly related to intangibles, and managers who do not have even a systematic language for looking at those processes will inevitably lag behind."

7 Sutcliff and Donnellan (2006), Chapter 5. Chapter 5 is entitled *"Enterprise performance management: Transforming finance in the journey to value-based management."*

8 Neely (2007), quoting from the Preface to the earlier (2001) edition of an edited volume on performance measurement, talked about: "New reports and articles on the topic [of performance measurement] ... appearing at a rate of every five hours of every working day since 1994." Neely then provided an updated assessment that as of September 2006, there were: "over 50,000,000 websites dedicated to performance measurement. ..." These include the very considerable literature relating to Quality Management or Business Excellence frameworks, indeed a very active area for many years, but very different from the topic addressed in this book. Nonetheless, the estimate appears to be somewhat higher than one might expect. The contributors to this book provide a number of references to the literature, but the volume as a whole does not constitute a complete coverage of the topic.

9 See *e.g.* Likierman (2009).

10 Fisher and Nair (2008).

11 Goldratt (1990).

12 Neely *et al.* (2007).

13 The original article was Kaplan and Norton (1992), and many subsequent books and journal articles (*e.g.* Kaplan and Norton 1996a, 1996b, 2006). Neely *et al.* (2007) reported that: "By 2001 the balanced scorecard had been adopted by 44 percent of organizations worldwide" although no data were provided to support such a remarkable statistic.

14 Subsequent publications by these and other authors have elaborated this approach in a variety of ways, for example, by describing scorecards that include environmental and people perspectives. For example, Huselid *et al.* (2005) describe an HR scorecard. However, that is as far as it goes.

There is no proposal for an overall system that helps put metrics in place that support priority-setting.

15 Atkinson *et al.* (1997) stated that:

"While we have no basic comment with this process approach to performance measurement, we feel that it is incomplete because it fails to:

- Adequately highlight the contributions employees and suppliers make to help the company achieve its objectives.
- Identify the role of the community in defining the environment within which the company works.
- Identify performance measurement as a two-way process, which enables management to assess stakeholders' contributions to the company's primary and secondary goals and enables stakeholders to assess whether the organization is capable of fulfilling its obligations to them now and in the future."

16 Various other writers have also noted the need to augment the scope of the Balanced Scorecard in terms of providing a Performance Measurement Framework, *e.g.* Otley (2007) and Neely *et al.* (2007).

17 Parmenter (2010) has developed an approach to Key Performance Indicators (KPIs) based on the Balanced Scorecard. The approach is almost completely *opposite* to the one advocated in this book. To take just two of the more striking examples:

1. "Many management books that cover KPIs talk about 'lead and lag indicators'; this merely clouds the KPI debate. Using the new way of looking at performance measures, we dispense with the terms *lag* (outcome) and *lead* (performance driver) indicators."

   This statement is completely discordant with best practice management frameworks. Parmenter's indicators depend significantly on measuring activity. This is a well-known trap in the Quality Management literature (and indeed, the literature for measuring research quality) as such measures are manipulated all too easily and can drive undesirable behaviors.

2. There is no focus on business processes in the book, let alone mention of the need to focus on improving business processes in order to improve KPIs.

18 Franco-Santos *et al.* (2007).

Acknowledgments

The origins of this book date back to the early 1990s, when I was confronted with the issue of what sorts of quantitative information I needed to run my research group.

I had encountered a compelling analogy: when I went to see my doctor for a check-up, he took a relatively small number of measurements, on the basis of which he was able to tell me about the current state of my health, where I was heading and what I needed to change to improve it. An organization is hardly a more complex organism than a human body. Why wasn't there any comparable information?

Thus began a lengthy odyssey. Initial advice from the leading Australian thinker in Quality Management, Norbert Vogel, led me to the United States to meet Myron Tribus; and through Myron, Homer Sarasohn, and Yoshikazu Tsuda in Japan; and then to Stockholm and Paris to talk to Richard Normann and his colleagues. An unrelated comment from my friend and colleague Bill Cleveland led me to meet Ray Kordupleski. In their various ways, these people had transformed industries, countries and business cultures. Each asked me difficult questions; each was remarkably generous with his time and ideas. And out of all these discussions emerged the overall shape of a performance measurement system centered on Stakeholder Value.

A basic framework was developed while I worked for CSIRO, and thoroughly tested by CSIRO colleagues. After I left CSIRO in mid-2001, the research into identifying and validating Stakeholder Value models was evaluated in case studies with a wide variety of businesses, large and small. Many people provided invaluable assistance along the way.

Clem Doherty suggested that the best way to get the system publicized was to write this book. Lourdes Llorens, Stephen Sasse and Brendan Donohue contributed extensively to validating the People Value model; Tony Peacock supported the development and testing of the Community Value model; Tony Press and Tessa Jakszewicz agreed to trial the Partner Value model; Ian Pollard was an invaluable sounding board when I was developing the concept of Owner Value, with David Gonski, John Deane, Greg L'Estrange, Russell Fountain, Frank Gooch and Peter Wolnizer also providing critical input.

Frank Blount, Robert Burke, Bill Cleveland, Tom Davenport, Peter Fitzgerald, Debby King-Rowley, Ray Kordupleski, Greg L'Estrange, David Morganstein, Ian Pollard, Stephen Sasse and Norbert Vogel provided insightful comments on various drafts of the book. Dan Lunn provided essential coaching in the use of CorelDraw to produce the exhibits. Michael King and Lisa Sarasohn kindly provided two photographs for the dedication.

Julian Cribb, Alan Lee, Ray Kordupleski, Peter Salmon and Norbert Vogel have, in their various ways, been excellent collaborators throughout the development of the research and the implementation and testing of the results in case studies.

To all these people, I offer my sincere thanks. Without their assistance, the system wouldn't have been created. Of course, any shortcomings in the resulting book are present despite their efforts.

I have made extensive use of Fisher Library at the University of Sydney, especially online. I thank the School of Mathematics and Statistics for my honorary appointment as Professor of Statistics since 2001, which has enabled access to this excellent resource.

I am most grateful to Paula Parish of Cambridge University Press for all her assistance in working with me to produce a convincing proposal to the Cambridge University Press Syndicate, and to Claire Poole for guiding the book through production. As always, Cambridge University Press has been an excellent collaborator in publishing ventures.

Finally, I thank my wife Lila for her love and support; firstly, for my decision to leave CSIRO so that I could test the methodology I was developing "in real life"; and secondly, because of the lengthy absences she has endured while I carried out the research for the book in various corners of the world.

N. I. Fisher
McMahons Point
2013

I How's *your* due diligence?

Managing on outcomes is like steering a car by looking in the rear view mirror.

Attributed to Myron Tribus

1.1 WHERE WERE WE?

Each of the pieces of information in Exhibit 1.1 relates to a real situation for a company or enterprise. Some of them were large, some small, some business and some governmental.

Most were associated with a disaster.

And each disaster could have been prevented by a Board requiring "appropriate" reporting of performance.

EXHIBIT 1.1. Welcome to the Board!

Welcome to the first meeting of the new Board of Golden Industries Group Inc.

As the new Chairman, I present to you a provisional first-quarter report for GIGI.

Following the company's recent scandal, several key employees have left and there's not much hard information available. In particular, we can't yet get any reliable financial reports.

However, I have prepared an interim report based on some summary data that the previous CEO had collected:

a. Share price up nearly three-fold in last six months
b. Payroll costs reduced by 10 percent
c. Acquisition of major competitor set for June
d. Record sales for a December quarter
e. 95 percent Customer Satisfaction achieved
f. April release of a new genetically modified crop
g. Annual staff survey score 3.8 (up from 3.6)
h. LTI (Lost Time Injury) 9.7 per 10^6 hours worked (down from 9.9)

What's the crux of the problem? In essence, in each case there was no *sound quantitative basis for making decisions*. While the various pieces of data looked good in isolation, each was misleading. For example,

a. The change in share price occurred during Al Dunlap's period as Chairman of Sunbeam.[1] The dramatic rise in Sunbeam's share price related more to major sales being brought forward, rather than to improved sales performance.

b. The reduction in payroll costs was a consequence of the departure of three key individuals in a knowledge-based enterprise.

c. AT&T acquired a competitor, NCR, without carrying out a prior Customer Value study to assess its relative market position.[2] Had they done so, the acquisition may well not have proceeded, at least not on the terms as negotiated.

d. Part of the Sunbeam story (*cf.* (a)): There were enormous increases in sales of electric blankets in the third quarter (of 1997), usually a fourth quarter phenomenon, and then of barbecues in the fourth quarter, when hardly anyone usually purchases them.

e. Part of the AT&T story (*cf.* (c)): Customer satisfaction was not being understood or assessed appropriately.[3]

f. A failure to measure and manage community concerns with genetically modified (GM) crops led to community rejection of GM food after very considerable investment in research and development (R&D).[4]

g. Data need to be available in a timely fashion to support appropriate preventative action. You can't wait several months to find out that there is sudden disenchantment in the workforce. Some of your best people may already have voted with their feet: see the case study in Chapter 5.

h. This wasn't a genuine decline: It was simply a random fluctuation in the measurement due to the limitations of sampling. There were, in fact, no grounds for reassurance about improvement in the level of safety, a critical issue for that company.

Our concern, in this book, is to describe a system that helps you guard against these sorts of problems that puts metrics in front of the leadership in a form that enables them to exercise due diligence in running the enterprise.

1.2 WHERE ARE WE NOW AND WHERE ARE WE HEADING?

If Exhibit 1.1 represents the performance measurement report from hell, what might you want from a good report? Here is a wish-list:

a. **The big picture**. Where are we now? What are the trends?
b. **Timely warning of emerging issues**. What issues are looming, that we can mitigate or avoid completely?
c. Assurance that all critical areas of the business are being covered.
d. **Actionable data**. Where do we need to focus attention, and why?
e. Capability to drill down when needed.

Where are we now? This information is provided in Exhibits 1.2 and 1.3, which should be interpreted as *electronic* reports. Between them, they cover all aspects of the business. Exhibit 1.2 shows the current situation with *some* key Owner metrics, mainly financial and risk indicators. We have chosen to use the context of a national retail group so that meaningful financial indicators can be provided. Features to note include:

- many financial indicators are *ratios*, to facilitate benchmarking;
- all indicators have associated trend charts;
- arrows indicate whether there has been any significant change since the last report; and
- overall Risk is assessed on the scale 0 (no risk) to 100 (maximum risk). The exclamation mark (!) indicates that a serious issue was detected at a lower level so the mark persists to the top-level report.

With this information, an overall picture of the current situation can be grasped very rapidly. For example:

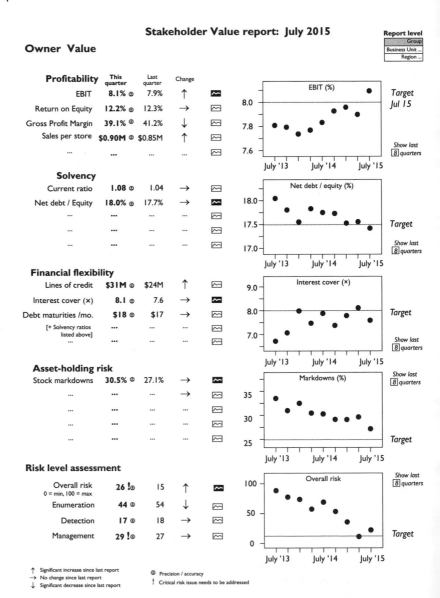

Stakeholder Value report: July 2015

Owner Value

Report level: Group / Business Unit ... / Region ...

Profitability

	This quarter	Last quarter	Change	
EBIT	8.1% ⊕	7.9%	↑	∿
Return on Equity	12.2% ⊕	12.3%	→	∿
Gross Profit Margin	39.1% ⊕	41.2%	↓	∿
Sales per store	$0.90M ⊕	$0.85M	↑	∿
...	...	...	...	∿

EBIT (%) — 8.0 — 7.8 — 7.6 — July '13, July '14, July '15 — Target Jul 15 — Show last 8 quarters

Solvency

Current ratio	1.08 ⊕	1.04	→	∿
Net debt / Equity	18.0% ⊕	17.7%	→	∿
...	...	...	...	∿
...	...	...	...	∿
...	...	...	...	∿

Net debt / equity (%) — 18.0 — 17.5 — 17.0 — July '13, July '14, July '15 — Target — Show last 8 quarters

Financial flexibility

Lines of credit	$31M ⊕	$24M	↑	∿
Interest cover (×)	8.1 ⊕	7.6	→	∿
Debt maturities /mo.	$18 ⊕	$17	→	∿
[+ Solvency ratios listed above]	...	...	...	∿
...	...	...	...	∿

Interest cover (×) — 9.0 — 8.0 — 7.0 — July '13, July '14, July '15 — Target — Show last 8 quarters

Asset-holding risk

Stock markdowns	30.5% ⊕	27.1%	→	∿
...	...	...	→	∿
...	...	...	...	∿
...	...	...	...	∿
...	...	...	...	∿

Markdowns (%) — 35 — 30 — 25 — July '13, July '14, July '15 — Target — Show last 8 quarters

Risk level assessment

Overall risk (0 = min, 100 = max)	26 !⊕	15	↑	∿
Enumeration	44 ⊕	54	↓	∿
Detection	17 ⊕	18	→	∿
Management	29 !⊕	27	→	∿

Overall risk — 100 — 50 — 0 — July '13, July '14, July '15 — Target — Show last 8 quarters

↑ Significant increase since last report
→ No change since last report
↓ Significant decrease since last report
⊕ Precision / accuracy
! Critical risk issue needs to be addressed

EXHIBIT 1.2. This exhibit contains top-level financial metrics and risk indicators for the Owner as stakeholder. Arrows denote significant movement since the previous report, trend charts are available for all measures. The icon ⊕ contains information about precision and accuracy of the corresponding performance metric. The alert (!) denotes a critical risk issue that arose at a lower level, and is forced to persist to the top level of reporting. The chart icon ∿ (dark when selected) is used to view a chart.

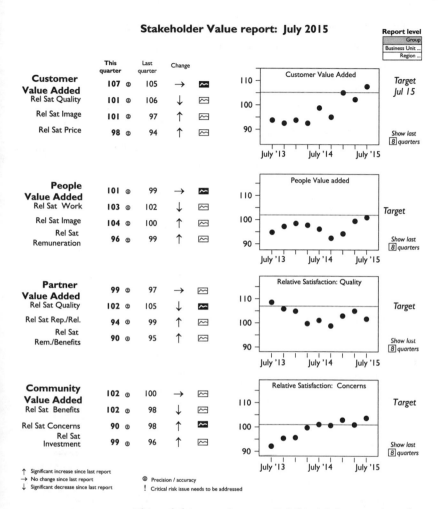

Stakeholder Value report: July 2015

EXHIBIT 1.3. This exhibit complements Exhibit 1.2, by providing the top-level measures for the other stakeholder groups. All scores are relative to 100 (par with the competition). The icon ⊕ contains information about precision and accuracy of the corresponding performance metric. (For such relative value scores, the precision is typically ± 2). Each relative value score has three drivers. Collectively, they capture the current position with all stakeholders (they are lag indicators).

- The financial indicators (Exhibit 1.2) reveal a satisfactory situation. The significant movement in EBIT over the last quarter has brought it up to the target level. The other financial indicators are at or about the targets set for the end of June.

- There has been steady and sustained improvement in overall management of Risk (last panel in Exhibit 1.2). However, there is an alert (!) of a critical issue and it derives from how a particular risk issue is being managed. The electronic nature of the report facilitates access to a short report (Exhibit 1.4(a)) to provide further explanation. This indicator is reserved for a mission-critical risk. It may have been detected at quite a low level in the enterprise, but is so serious that it must be drawn to the Board's attention, so it cannot be erased from the system except at Board level: the warning must persist in all higher-level reports.

- The enterprise has performed strongly in the marketplace over the last year (first panel of Exhibit 1.3) and is in a dominant position

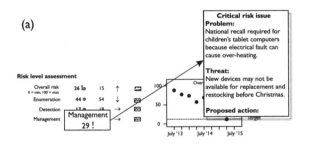

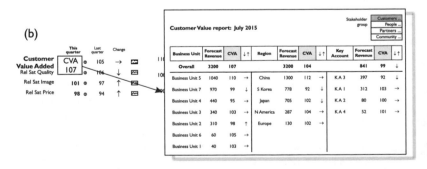

EXHIBIT 1.4. Reports provide the capability to drill down. (a) The Risk Management alert in Exhibit 1.2 has an associated note providing relevant details. (b) The high Customer Value Added score in Exhibit 1.3 can be studied in more detail by looking at an associated report, showing CVA scores by Business Unit, Region or Key Account.

despite an overall drop in perceived Quality, relative to the competition. Exhibit 1.4(b) reveals greater detail about where the excellent performance is occurring.

- An improved performance with People over the last year has the enterprise close to its target, which was slightly above par.
- Relationships with Partners are consistently below the target the enterprise had set for itself, and some sort of specific intervention might be required.
- A committed two-year effort to improving the relationship with the Community appears to have worked well.

These exhibits tell the Board where things are now. To the extent that they are good numbers, they are measuring the success of past efforts by the enterprise to create and add superior Value for all stakeholders.

However, the more interesting question is:

Where is the enterprise heading, and where should it focus its improvement activities?

For this, we need corresponding sets of *lead indicators*.

Exhibits 1.5 and 1.6 show indicative related reports for Owners and for other stakeholders, respectively, to provide a flavor of the sorts of actionable data you need to operate diligently as a leader. As far as financial indicators are concerned, we need to be somewhat specific about the industry sector, as there can be enormous sectoral variation in indicator benchmark values.

Again, the key information in Exhibits 1.5 and 1.6 is readily accessible for leadership. For example,

- From Exhibit 1.5, *Consumer sentiment* is trending up (allowing for a seasonal effect), a good lead indicator for EBIT. The trends in Debtor Days (lead indicator for Net debt/equity), Share price (Lines of Credit) and Unforseen events classified as "high risk" (Overall Risk) are also in the right direction.

Key Performance Indicator report: July 2015

Report level

Group	
Business Unit ...	
Region ...	

Lead indicators for Financial and Risk metrics

Profitability	This quarter	Last quarter	Change		
Unemployment rate	5.5% ⊕	5.6%	→	〰	
Market share	45.4 ⊕	42.1	↑	〰	
Consumer sentiment	101 ⊕	110	→	〰	
Unplanned staff turnover	9.4% ⊕	11.1%	↓	〰	
...	...	...	...	〰	

Consumer sentiment — Par — Show last 12 quarters (July '12, July '13, July '14, July '15)

Solvency					
Cashflow forecast	3.5 ⊕	3.4	→	〰	
Debtor days	24 ⊕	22	→	〰	
...	...	...	...	〰	
...	...	...	...	〰	
...	...	...	...	〰	

Debtor days — Target Jul '15 — Show last 12 quarters (July '12, July '13, July '14, July '15)

Financial flexibility

	This quarter	Last quarter	Change		
Share price	$4.72 ⊕	$4.62	→	〰	
Interest cover	8.5 ⊕	8.2	→	〰	
...	...	...	...	〰	
...	...	...	...	〰	
...	...	...	...	〰	

Share price ($) — Show last 12 quarters (July '12, July '13, July '14, July '15)

Asset-holding risk

	This quarter	Last quarter	Change		
% Inventory > 3mo.	14.8% ⊕	15.1%	→	〰	
...	...	...	...	〰	
...	...	...	...	〰	
...	...	...	...	〰	
...	...	...	...	〰	

Inventory > 3mo. (%) — Show last 12 quarters — Target Jul '15 (July '12, July '13, July '14, July '15)

Risk level assessment

	This quarter	Last quarter	Change		
*Class One Event freq.	$1.5/10^5$h ⊕	$1.4/10^5$h	→	〰	
% unforeseen events classified 'high-risk'	2.2% ⊕	3.1%	↓	〰	
% complete problem-free audits	97% ⊕	91%	↑	〰	
% compliance with statutory reporting	91% ⊕	81%	↑	〰	

Unforeseen events classified 'high-risk' (%) — Show last 8 quarters — Target (July '13, July '14, July '15)

↑ Significant increase since last report
→ No change since last report
↓ Significant decrease since last report

* How often we create an environment where someone is, or reasonably could have been, killed or injured

EXHIBIT 1.5. The purpose of the indicators in Exhibits 1.5 and 1.6 is to help predict where the enterprise is heading, to enable the leadership to take action in anticipation of problems, and also to capitalize on emerging opportunities. Note how trends in individual graphs in Exhibit 1.5 anticipate corresponding trends in Exhibit 1.2. The indicators in Exhibit 1.5 relate to the financial and risk management aspects of the business.

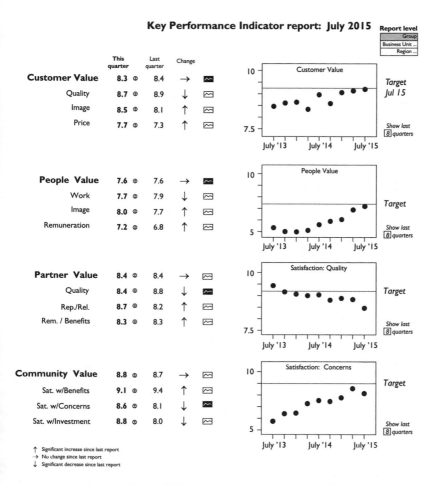

EXHIBIT 1.6. This exhibit complements Exhibit 1.5, by providing
lead indicators for the other stakeholder groups. All scores are ratings
on the scale 1 (Poor) to 10 (Excellent). They are the current ratings
for your enterprise, whereas those in Exhibit 1.4 are measured
relative to your competitors.

- For the category *Asset-holding risk*, Age of inventory has started to
  increase again, which may not augur well for future *Stock
  markdowns*.
- From Exhibit 1.6, we conclude that the enterprise is steadily
  improving its position as far as *Customers* and the *Community* are
  concerned.

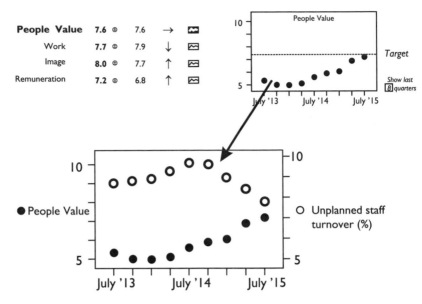

People Value	7.6 ⊕	7.6	→	〰	
Work	7.7 ⊕	7.9	↓	〰	
Image	8.0 ⊕	7.7	↑	〰	
Remuneration	7.2 ⊕	6.8	↑	〰	

EXHIBIT 1.7. People Value as a lead indicator of Unplanned staff turnover. It is usually helpful to produce lead and lag indicators on the same graph so that the nature of the relationship can be appreciated, which can then be validated by statistical modeling and analysis.

- *People Value* was at a very low point, but now appears to be improving steadily. If *Unplanned staff turnover* data are available, we would expect to see the sort of pattern shown in Exhibit 1.7: as People Value increases, after a lag of a few quarters, Unplanned staff turnover starts to decrease.
- There is an issue with Partner Value, where the overall Quality of the Partner relationships has been declining steadily for two years. It hasn't yet reached the point of being flagged as a mission-critical risk, but something clearly needs to be done.

So, how do you decide which numbers *you* actually need? That is what is discussed over the next several chapters. The goal is to develop a set of metrics that provides a concise yet comprehensive view of the current situation and where you are heading; in other words, a set of numbers that will provide assurance to you, your colleagues and your shareholders that you are being duly diligent.

NOTES

1 The Sunbeam story is documented in many places, *e.g.* Byrne (1998).
2 For a more complete story see Kordupleski (2003), pages 51, 311.
3 See *Ibid.*, pages xv–xvii. Likierman (2009) nominates "Measuring against yourself" as his first "trap," which was one of AT&T's mistakes.
4 From Cribb and Sari (2009): "During the 1990s and early 2000s, a wave of hostile public sentiment emerged in both developed and developing countries towards GM foods. This was more pronounced in some countries than in others, but was dramatic enough for some international investment houses to advise their clients to sell off their biotech shares and for a great many transgenic research programs to be terminated."

2 Introduction to the system

2.1 PURPOSE

The goal of this book is to describe a system for performance measurement that gives you quantitative information that you can trust to help you run your enterprise.

When we talk about "quantitative information that you can trust" we mean information that is:

- timely
- actionable – in a format (graphical or tabular) that facilitates decision-making
- measures the right thing, the right way
- clearly interpretable in terms of its limitations – degree of uncertainty in the measurement, possible biases.

What should a good measurement system provide? Exhibit 2.1 summarizes the essentials.[1]

Ideally, the concise overview will be:

EXHIBIT 2.1. The critical outcomes that should be provided by a system for measuring the performance of an enterprise.

1. A concise overview of the health of your enterprise.
2. A quantitative basis for selecting improvement priorities.
3. Alignment of the efforts of the people with the mission of the enterprise.

- *Comprehensive*: it will cover all aspects of the enterprise – your markets, your people, your suppliers and partners, and the wider community – not just the financials;
- *Current*: it will tell you how things are going at present, on all fronts; and

- *Predictive*: it will provide reliable forecasts of likely future performance in all areas.

Concision also matters. The only thing worse than too little data is too much data. Here, Price's Dictum[2] comes to the rescue:

- No inspection or measurement without proper recording.
- No recording without analysis.
- No analysis without action.

This advice originated in an engineering context but has wide applicability, not least in keeping leadership reports to a parsimonious minimum.

How will you judge which improvement priorities to select? The most obvious criterion is to look at their predicted impact on your business, either directly on the bottom line, or indirectly through their impact on a major driver of bottom-line performance such as market share or staff turnover.

Alignment involves not just the individual metrics people use in their work and how these encourage working to a common purpose, but also alignment of the metrics used at all levels of the enterprise.

How do we go about building a system that captures these essentials? Well, think about designing a car. You need designs for two basic elements:

- the carriage-work, and
- the engine.

It's the same for the performance measurement system: there are two requirements, as shown in Exhibit 2.2.

EXHIBIT 2.2. Two basic components of a performance measurement system. Put another way, the first requirement states that you need a *structure* for performance measures.

Requirement 1: a way to identify the sorts of data that are needed.
Requirement 2: a way of putting the actual measures in place, and using them to best effect.

The second requirement states that you need measures that help you to do things like addressing your most pressing business issues, *e.g.* excessive production costs, falling market share, high staff turnover, lack of community support for a development.

So that's what we'll be doing in the following pages: designing a measurement system to transport your enterprise where you hope to go, and in the style that you'd like to travel.

2.2   FINANCIAL AND NON-FINANCIAL METRICS

One important thing you will have noticed already is the lack of attention paid to *financial* metrics. Of course, financial metrics are essential. However, knowledge in this area is very widespread and accessible.

Instead, the emphasis in this book will be on *non-financial* metrics. There is abundant evidence that good management of so-called "intangible assets," even narrowly defined, contributes significantly to improved financial performance and enhanced market value for an enterprise.[3] Davenport and Harris note that[4]

> Nonfinancial or intangible resources (such as human knowledge capital, brand, R&D capability) are growing in importance to both company business performance and external perceptions of company value. Even the most favourable studies show an explanatory power of approximately 50% for the effect of financial measures such as earnings per share, net income, economic profit, or return on invested capital on a company's market value.

Davenport and Harris describe how quickly poor company fortunes were able to be turned around by broadening the focus from purely financial to both financial and non-financial metrics.

Twenty years ago, Robert Eccles observed that[5]

> Not surprisingly, methods for measuring financial performance are the most sophisticated and deeply entrenched ….

> In contrast, efforts to measure market share, quality, innovation, human resources, and customer satisfaction have been much more modest. Data for tracking these measures are

generated less often: quarterly, annual, or even biannual bases are common.

Responsibility for tracking them typically rests with a specific function ... they rarely become part of the periodic reports general managers receive.

Placing *these new measures on an equal footing with financial data takes significant resources.* One approach is to assign a senior executive to each of the measures and hold him or her responsible for developing its methodologies. (Emphasis added.)

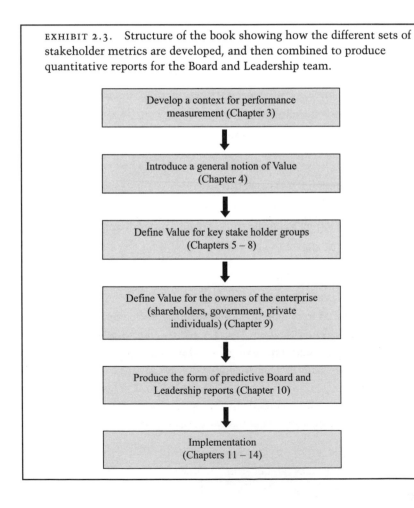

EXHIBIT 2.3.   Structure of the book showing how the different sets of stakeholder metrics are developed, and then combined to produce quantitative reports for the Board and Leadership team.

Develop a context for performance measurement (Chapter 3)

Introduce a general notion of Value (Chapter 4)

Define Value for key stake holder groups (Chapters 5 – 8)

Define Value for the owners of the enterprise (shareholders, government, private individuals) (Chapter 9)

Produce the form of predictive Board and Leadership reports (Chapter 10)

Implementation (Chapters 11 – 14)

More recently, Ray Kordupleski was able to assert, in a passage headed *Losing Sleep over Customer Data*, that

> there is an emerging art and science of customer value management that is proving its worth in increasing market share and shareholder value for the companies that practice it. Companies that capture and use customer data with the same kind of discipline, passion and understanding they give to the operational and financial data are learning that this business practice is well worth the time and money invested.[6]

Thus, non-financial metrics are an essential complement to financial metrics in providing leadership with the means to gain and sustain competitive success.

In the previous chapter, we had a glimpse of how the two sets of metrics fit together into comprehensive, concise and predictive reports for the Board and Leadership team. In the subsequent chapters, we show how the reports are derived. The overall plan for our discussion is shown in Exhibit 2.3.

NOTES

1 Atkinson *et al.* (2007), in discussing their stakeholder-based approach to strategic performance measurement, take a different perspective. They comment (page 30):

"we believe that a performance measurement system must do four things:

1. Help the company evaluate whether it is receiving the expected contributions from employees and suppliers, the elements of its internal stakeholder group, and the expected returns from customer groups. ... This element relates to *value received* from suppliers and employees.
2. Help the company evaluate whether it is giving each stakeholder group what it needs to continue to contribute so the company can meet its primary objectives....This element relates to *value provided* to the stakeholders.
3. Guide the design and implementation of processes that contribute to the company's secondary objectives. ... This element relates to *process efficiency*.

4. Help the company evaluate its planning and the contracts, both implicit and explicit, that it negotiated with the stakeholders by helping it evaluate the effect of secondary objectives on its primary objectives. . . . This . . . relates to the company's *strategic properties*."

Whilst there is some measure of agreement between the desiderata in Exhibit 1.2 and those listed here, there are also significant differences, reflecting the different ways that stakeholders are viewed. In our framework, value needs to be created and added for all stakeholder groups, in a competitive environment.

That said, a subsequent comment (*ibid.*, page 30) is entirely consistent with our view: "The contributions and requirements that a company negotiates with each group and the contribution that each process makes to achieving the secondary objectives defines the focus of the performance measurement system . . ."

In the context of performance measurement systems for public sector organizations, Goh (2012, page 38) argues that: "a performance measurement system that encourages the use of results for learning and improvement is the key to having an effective overall performance measurement system in a public sector organization. The previous discussion in the paper . . . suggests that there are three critical factors that need to be integrated into an effective performance measurement system. They are: stakeholder involvement, a learning and evaluative organizational culture and managerial discretion."

The system described in this book is consistent with these requirements.

2 See Price (1984).
3 See the article "Future Value: The $7 trillion challenge" by Ballow *et al.* (2004). A detailed classification of Assets into *Tangible* and *Intangible*, and cross-classified at *Traditional* and *Intellectual*, is given on page 32. Future value, "that portion of a stock's price that does not depend on current operating performance but rather on the company's anticipated growth," derives from intangible assets, such as credit ratings, customer loyalty, knowledge and know-how, brand image, staff loyalty, community support, esteem of peer enterprises and current and prospective partners, *etc.*
4 Davenport and Harris (2007), pages 61–2.
5 Eccles (1991).
6 Kordupleski (2003), page xiv.

3   A framework for performance measurement

> We intend to conduct our business in a way that not only meets but
> exceeds the expectations of our customers, business partners,
> shareholders, and creditors, as well as the communities in which we
> operate and society at large.

Akira Mori

3.1   PREAMBLE ON DEVELOPING MEASUREMENT STRATEGIES

How do we work out what sorts of measures are needed to help run an
enterprise? We'll use three methods.

One reasonable starting point is to decide on some *principles*
for selecting performance measures. It's not only reasonable, it's
important because poorly chosen measures can distort people's
behavior, with disastrous and expensive consequences, as we'll see
shortly.

Then there's a simple way of thinking about *how* to identify
measures that can help you find your way, even in the foggiest circumstances. It's the Tribus Paradigm, named after a very clear and
practical thinker about management: Myron Tribus.

Finally, it's important to recognize that there's a *hierarchy*
amongst performance measures: indeed, the Tribus Paradigm leads
us inexorably to a performance measurement structure.

So that's the Framework that will now be developed: a set of
Principles for selecting measures, a *Paradigm* for thinking about
which performance measures are needed, and a *structure* for performance measures.

3.2   THE PRINCIPLES

> **The First Principle: Alignment**
> The enterprise's approach to measurement encourages alignment of people and systems with the organization's mission, vision and goals.

How do you respond to the enquiry: "What is your job?"

This simple question goes to a core issue of performance measurement: understanding and distinguishing between what you're *accountable* for and what you're *responsible* for. The distinction is what will help you decide:

a. what measures you need for reporting purposes; and
b. what measures should be reported to you.

Let's start at the top of the enterprise. The Chief Executive Officer (CEO) is charged by the Board with running the enterprise – production, marketing, sales, resource management, budgeting, planning *etc.* All of these are the CEO's areas of Accountability.

Of course, superhuman though they may be, CEOs can't do all this work themselves. In fact, almost everything is delegated, together with the authority to make decisions about delegated activities. What's left, which is the stuff that won't get done if the CEO doesn't come to work, constitutes the CEO's actual areas of Responsibility.

However, the CEO needs to report against the areas of Accountability. *Accountability cannot be delegated.*

All of this seems obvious. Yet ignorance of the distinction between Accountability and Responsibility, and attempts to delegate – in effect, to deny – Accountability, are legion and can be very significant. For example:

• The captain of the *Exxon Valdez* oil tanker, which created a massive oil spill that became one of the great man-made environmental disasters at sea, was not held fully accountable for the disaster.[1]

- Unauthorized trading by a head derivatives trader, Nick Leeson, led to the collapse of Barings Bank in 1995.[2]
- When Homer Sarasohn was teaching Japanese communications executives about Quality Management in 1949, he found that the Japanese had no concept of Accountability (and hence no word for it in their language).[3]

So, provided that your areas of Accountability as CEO relate to the mission of your enterprise, *and the measures that you report relate appropriately to these areas*, you have created Alignment for yourself.

By appropriate delegation of Responsibility and Authority, you begin to spread Alignment of people with purpose down through your enterprise. Again, the measures that they report *need to relate appropriately* to their areas of Accountability.

We shall return to this awkward little term "relate appropriately" in the next chapter. For the moment, let's note just a few examples of unfortunate situations where the measures chosen did *not* relate appropriately:

- A British firm involved in manufacture of toys. In one room, the people who were assembling toys were being paid by the number assembled per hour. In the next room, the inspectors were being paid according to the number of defects they found. After a short while, of course, people in the two rooms started talking to each other and developed a common goal – but not one that was aligned with the purpose of the enterprise.
- A similar example on a grander scale occurred at Motorola, when they began to focus on a single metric, cycle time, to drive all improvements. The consequence was a reduction in cycle time, but at tremendous cost of quality, as the faster processes were leading to a lot of rework. This resulted in the introduction of a second metric: an insistence that these processes also be capable of meeting customer requirements almost all the time (less than one failure in a million). And so was born the so-called "Six Sigma" approach.[4]

- A survey of travelers on the suburban train system in Sydney identified "on time arrival" as an important customer requirement. As a result, train drivers were given a performance target of "95% on-time arrivals at stations." However, there was no further requirement that trains actually stopped to allow passengers to board or leave the train.

- The problems at Sunbeam (*cf.* Section 1.1) could be traced in part to the leader being rewarded on the basis of quarterly performance.

> You tell me how you measure me, and I will tell you how I will behave.
>
> *Eliyahu Goldratt*

> Hold everyone accountable? Ridiculous!
>
> *W. Edwards Deming*

What about alignment of processes and systems?

In large part, that's the subject of the next five chapters. However, it's also part of the paradigm for selecting measures that we'll discuss shortly.

Meanwhile, to round out the discussion of Alignment, we visit an ancient management cartoon (Exhibit 3.1), which provides a simple analogy for what a good performance management system should achieve.

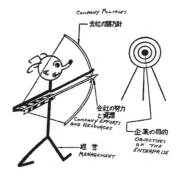

EXHIBIT 3.1. A cartoon drawn by Homer Sarasohn in the training manual used to teach Management to top Japanese just after the Second World War. The accompanying caption read: *The policies created by management must direct the efforts and resources of the company to a defined target – the fundamental objectives of the enterprise.*

> The Second Principle: Process and systems thinking
> Measures should be linked appropriately with system and process
> monitoring, control and improvement.

> If you can't describe what you are doing as a process, you don't
> know what you are doing.
>
> *W. Edwards Deming*

This is almost self-evident: the way to improve the outcome is to improve the process or system that produces it.

Output and outcome measures can tell you whether you've done a good job. These can be relatively easy to come by. They relate to your areas of Accountability.

Appropriate process and system measures will tell you something that may be far more important: that you're on track to do a good or better job in the future. These may be rather harder to produce, and relate to what you should be monitoring for your areas of Accountability.

> The Third Principle: Practicability
> At any level in the enterprise, there is a straightforward procedure for
> identifying the sorts of measures that need to be collected, and what
> needs to be reported.

Again, a simple requirement: when you decide to introduce performance measurement systematically, what's wanted is a simple and robust implementation process that is led from within and replicable in its approach throughout the enterprise, rather than an expensive and disruptive intervention led by a team of external consultants.

3.3   THE PARADIGM

If you're wondering what you can be measuring that will help you with your work, no matter whether you're the CEO or the person on the front desk, the Tribus Paradigm will get you out of jail every time.

The Tribus Paradigm

1. What products or services are produced and for whom?
2. How will "quality," or "excellence" of the product or service be assessed and how can this be measured?
3. Which processes produce these products and services?
4. What has to be measured to forecast whether a satisfactory level of quality will be attained?   – after Myron Tribus

---

You'll see it being applied repeatedly over the next several chapters. More immediately, it provides a lead-in to our next topic, the third component of the Performance Measurement Framework. Where do we start when we want to identify performance measures?

3.4 A STRUCTURE FOR PERFORMANCE MEASURES

Ready. Fire. Aim.

Anon.

Impact. Outcome. Success. Where do all these things take place?

They take place in the outside world – outside your enterprise, that is. So that's the starting point for measuring the performance of your enterprise,

Zones of Measurement

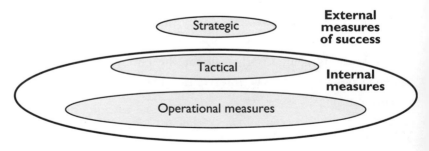

EXHIBIT 3.2. The three Zones of Measurement, corresponding to Sarasohn's Zones of Management. In accordance with the Tribus Paradigm, the starting point for measurement is outside the enterprise: its success or otherwise is judged by its impact on the outside world.

and it's also how to interpret the first line of the Tribus Paradigm. The outside world is the Strategic Zone of Measurement[5] in Exhibit 3.2.

You don't get to mark your own examination paper to find out how successful you've been. It's judged by others. What you do get to control are the *Tactical and Operational Zones*, which we'll look at shortly. First, however, what goes on in the Strategic Zone?

The Strategic Zone of Measurement

This zone contains all the different stakeholders for whom your enterprise aims to produce *beneficial outcomes*. It's convenient to divide them into five groups – Owners of the business, Customers, People, Partners, and the Community – as shown in Exhibit 3.3. We'll use the term *Success Measures* to describe performance measurements in this zone. This zone is the province of the Board of your enterprise.[6]

The contention is that each of the groups is basically a market in which you compete. You're inviting each stakeholder to make some form of investment in your enterprise: *Owners*, their resources; *People*, their labor; *Customers* their money; *Partners*, their resources and cooperation; and the *Community*, their sanction and support. They will only do this if they perceive that you're offering more

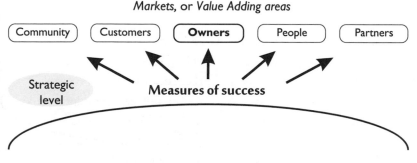

EXHIBIT 3.3. The Strategic Zone comprises five groups of stakeholders. Success Measures capture the value of the stakeholder's investment (resources, money, labor, *etc.*) in your enterprise, compared with an alternative investment. The contention is that your enterprise needs to win in all markets to ensure sustainable success.

Value[7] than they can get somewhere else, *and they all have alternative choices for their investments.*

There's your challenge: to offer superior Value to all the stakeholders. So who are all these people, and are they all equally important? That seems like a lot of people who need to be kept happy.

The *Owners* are the easiest group to describe: they provide the funding and receive the returns – although the returns are not necessarily financial. For a publicly listed company, the shareholders hope to receive returns in the form of dividends and growth of their investment, whereas for a government enterprise the government hopes to be re-elected.

In contrast, the *Customer* market (*i.e.* current and prospective customers) can be very complex. Let's consider two rather different examples:

- A large diversified electronics enterprise with a wide range of offerings: products (computers, mobile phones, game boxes *etc.*), and services (music downloads, movie downloads *etc.*). *Market segmentation* is needed to identify the different sub-groups on the basis of their diverse needs. Once that's been done, the processes for defining and creating Value for each of these groups are quite similar.
- A regional government authority, the Port Stephens Council in New South Wales, Australia, is responsible for an area that includes beaches, wilderness areas, wine-growing regions and industrial zones. A *stakeholder analysis* would then identify an extraordinary diversity of sub-groups with conflicting sets of requirements: residents, local businessmen, tourists, developers, environmentalists *etc.* Not only are the processes for defining and creating Value quite different; there's also an issue of balancing the relative importance of each of these sub-groups. Which ones are really vital to the long-term survival of a council?
- *People* refers to those who currently work for your enterprise, and those whom you'd like to employ. Again, there are sub-groups with

differing requirements. However, as we'll see, the processes for
defining and creating Value for each of these groups are quite similar.

- *Partners* come in various forms. A supplier of components or
  services would fall into this category. So would an enterprise with
  whom you're partnering on a particular project. And then there's a
  partnership for an indefinite period of time, a co-venture in which
  the collaboration is fundamentally strategic. These different types
  of partnership would have very different concepts of Value, and very
  different processes would be needed to deliver Value.

- The *Community* can also mean very different things. If you're
  planning to build a chemical factory in a partly residential area, the
  Community would comprise people living close enough to be
  affected by your presence. In contrast, if you plan to manage plagues
  of pest mice destroying crops by a country-wide release of a GM
  virus, with the intention of making female mice infertile, then you
  can expect that the whole country will take an interest. Will the
  virus jump species and affect their pets? Will it affect humans? Will
  crops supposedly protected by this means be acceptable to overseas
  trading partners opposed to GM methods?

All of this flows from the first line of the Tribus Paradigm: What
products or services are produced and for whom? You have a wide
range of stakeholders, all with a vested interest in the success of your
enterprise.[8] And it will be their *perceptions* that determine whether or
not you've succeeded.

In other words, the highest level metrics in the performance
measurement system are perceptual: they are so-called "soft" – or
subjective – numbers, rather than "hard" – or objective – numbers.

And the final point is: *you have to deliver superior Value to all
of the stakeholder groups, to achieve and sustain long-term success.*
In the short term, you may get away with poor customer service,
ignoring your employees' requests for better pay and conditions, not
keeping your relationship with a key partner in good shape, or ignoring the community's protests about emissions from your factory or

traffic problems at the entrance to your plant. In the long term, however, these will come back to bite you.

The Tactical Zone of Measurement

Management is Prediction.

W. Edwards Deming

The top level of performance measures indicates how successful you've been with your various stakeholder groups. *However, you can't manage with these measures*: all they are telling you is what's happened as a consequence of your past activities. Recall the quote from Myron Tribus: *Managing on outcomes is like steering a car by looking in the rear view mirror.*

For management purposes, what you really need are performance measures that will forecast where you're heading; in other words, *that predict likely future values of the Success Measures.*

We call these measures *Key Performance Indicators* (KPIs); see Exhibit 3.4. They are the province of your Leadership team. Specifically, KPIs relate to Leaderships' areas of Accountability and Responsibility, although most of the Responsibilities will have been delegated. They provide the basis for regular reports to the Board and Leadership team.

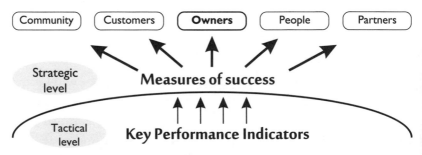

EXHIBIT 3.4. The Tactical Zone comprises a set of Key Performance Indicators, which are enterprise-level measures used by the leadership to help manage the enterprise. They are lead indicators of Success Measures. They form a vital core component of regular Board and Leadership reports.

KPIs may take two forms. Some will be system-level measures that monitor how the management system promotes integration of the strategic intent of your enterprise with its products, services and processes. Others may be aggregated measures of operational performance, relating to a manager's area of Accountability.

While there is no requirement that KPIs be comparative in nature (in contrast to Success Measures), it is common practice for high-performing enterprises to use "benchmarking" against industry standards to calibrate their KPIs.

The Operational Zone of Measurement

The word "Operational" relates to the processes in which the people of the enterprise interact to create its Value Added products and services. Therefore, operational measures relate to process, product and service performance, and form the basis for improvement activities; see Exhibit 3.5.

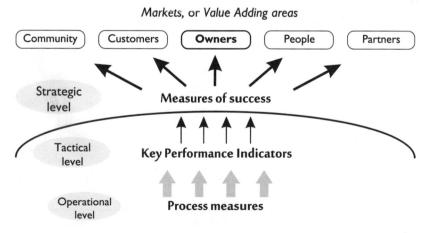

EXHIBIT 3.5. The Operational Zone contains all the measures relating to monitoring, controlling and improving the processes that deliver products and services to stakeholders. Operational measures have time frames from instantaneous to (typically short-term) aggregations, and are determined from the specific characteristics of the products and services through quality requirements, specifications, and process procedures and standards. Hence, these measures relate to direct control and are specific to the product or service process.

They include lead and lag indicators, and relate to people's Accountabilities and Responsibilities.

And they can be of concern to top management! Toyota's massive worldwide recall of cars in 2010[9] was due to poor performance on low-level quality attributes of accelerator pedals. The corresponding lead indicators would – or at least, should – appear on well-constructed Board and senior leadership reports (see Chapter 10). If you can't "go to *gemba*," as the Japanese have it (meaning "go to where the action is," in this case the factory floor where brake pedals are being manufactured and tested), then at least ensure that your regular reports are a good surrogate for *gemba*.

3.5   FINAL COMMENTS ON THE PERFORMANCE MEASUREMENT FRAMEWORK

Exhibit 3.6 summarizes the three components of the Performance Measurement Framework:

This tells us what we need in the way of measures and goes some way to meeting the three criteria[10] laid down in the previous chapter (Exhibit 2.1):

- a concise overview of the health of your enterprise;
- a quantitative basis for selecting improvement priorities; and
- alignment of the efforts of the people with the mission of the enterprise.

Now we need to look at the second requirement in Exhibit 2.2: a means of putting appropriate measures in place and using them to

---

EXHIBIT 3.6.   The Performance Measurement Framework in summary.

- Three Principles, relating to the need for Alignment, Process and Systems focus, and Practicality.
- The Tribus Paradigm for thinking about what to measure.
- A Structure for performance measures, with three Zones of Measurement – Strategic, Tactical and Operational.

run the enterprise. In other words, we need to populate the different Zones of Measurement, starting with measuring *Success*, or *Value provided to stakeholders*.

So, what do we mean by Stakeholder Value?

NOTES

1 The *Exxon Valdez* oil tanker struck Bligh Reef in the Prince William Sound, Alaska, on March 24, 1989, resulting in a massive oil spill that became one of the great man-made environmental disasters at sea. The captain was not on the bridge at the time. In the subsequent trial, he was convicted of a misdemeanor charge of negligent discharge of oil, but not held fully accountable for the disaster.

2 As described in *The New York Times* of 19 July, 1995: "Under Barings Futures Singapore's management structure through 1995, Leeson doubled as both the floor manager for Barings' trading on the Singapore International Monetary Exchange and head of settlement operations. In the latter role, he was charged with ensuring accurate accounting for the unit. The positions would normally have been held by two different employees. As trading floor manager, Leeson reported to the head of settlement operations, an office inside Barings Bank which he himself held, which short-circuited normal accounting and internal control/audit safeguards. In effect, Leeson was able to operate with no supervision from London. After the collapse, several observers, including Leeson himself, placed much of the blame on the bank's own deficient internal auditing and risk management practices. Rather than the large profits the management of Barings thought were being posted in Singapore, the Bank of England's report showed that Mr. Leeson's operation lost money almost from the beginning. By the end of 1993, those losses totaled £20 million, rising to more than £200 million by the end of 1994 and escalating to £827 million ($1.3 billion) by the end of February. While faulting Mr. Leeson for a 'complex and systematic process of deception and false accounting,' the report also lambasted the executives above him. 'No one within Barings accepted responsibility for Leeson for the whole of 1994,' Mr. Clarke said."

3 The Japanese had a very well-developed sense of Responsibility and the honorable consequences of failure to discharge their Responsibilities properly. However, the notion that they could delegate a task to

someone else, yet should that person fail in the task they themselves would remain accountable for the failure was, initially, shocking to them. Sarasohn actually introduced the word "Accountability" into the Japanese language (having first taught himself Japanese). More details of Sarasohn's activities in Japan can be found in Fisher (2009). To this day, it is not easy to make the distinction between the two concepts of *Accountability* and *Responsibility* in languages as diverse as those of Spain and the Republic of Korea.

4 For more details see Fisher and Nair (2008).

5 These correspond to the three Zones of Management described by, for example, Sarasohn and Protzman (1948), Chapter II, but the term quite possibly predates this usage.

6 The importance of the stakeholder focus is also reflected in current Business Excellence frameworks, such as those of Baldrige and the European Foundation for Quality Management.

7 The concept of Value Adding was introduced by the leading strategic management thinker Richard Normann in the 1970s. Lerro (2011) provides a review of literature of stakeholder-focused approaches to management via added Value.

8 There is considerable divergence of views in the literature about why an enterprise exists, and what its purpose should be.

On the one hand, Goldratt (1990) states categorically that the goal of any company whose shares are traded in the open market is to use invested money to make more money now and in the future.

In contrast, in the opening chapter of his notes on industrial management (Sarasohn and Protzman, 1948), Homer Sarasohn wrote:

"Why does any company exist? What is the reason for being of any business enterprise? Many people would probably answer these questions by saying that the purpose of a company is to make a profit. In fact, if I were to ask you to write down right now the principal reason why your companies are in business, I suppose that most of the answers would be something of this sort.

"But such a statement is not a complete idea, nor is it a satisfactory answer because it does not clearly state the objective of the company, the principal goal that the company management is to strive for. A company's objective should be stated in a way which will not permit of any uncertainty as to its real fundamental purpose. For example, there are two ways of looking at that statement about profit. One is to make the product for a cost that is less than the price at which it is to be sold. The other is to sell the product for a price higher than it costs to make.

"These two views are almost the same – but not quite. The first implies a cost-conscious attitude on the part of the company. The second seems to say whatever the product costs, it will be sold at a higher price.

"There is another fault that I would find in such a statement. It is entirely selfish and one–sided. It ignores entirely the sociologic aspects that should be a part of a company's thinking. The business enterprise must be founded upon a sense of responsibility to the public and to its employees. Service to its customers, the wellbeing of its employees, good citizenship in the communities in which it operates – these are cardinal principles fundamental to any business. They provide the platform upon which a profitable company is built.

"The founder of the Newport News Shipbuilding and Dry Dock Company, when he was starting his company many years ago, wrote down his idea of the objective – the purpose – of the enterprise.

"He put it this way. 'We shall build good ships here; at a profit if we can – at a loss if we must – but, always good ships.'

"This is the guiding principle of this company and its fundamental policy. And it is a good one too because in a very few words it tells the whole reason for the existence of the enterprise. And yet inherent in these few words there is a wealth of meaning. The determination to put quality ahead of profit. A promise to stay in business in spite of adversity. A determination to find the best production methods."

W. Edwards Deming, writing much later when he was expounding his theory of Profound Knowledge, wrote that: "The aim proposed here for any organization is for everybody to gain – stockholders, employees, suppliers, customers, community, the environment – over the long term." (Deming 1994, page 51.)

Ray Kordupleski comments, in his opening chapter (Kordupleski 2003) that: "I used to think that winning in the financial market should be a company's main focus – that businesses exist to create value for shareholders. Over the years, I've come to realize I was looking at things the wrong way. *I now believe businesses have a greater chance of thriving over the long term if they think of shareholder value as the reward, not the purpose.*" (Emphasis added.)

And recently, Elisabeth Murdoch, Chair of television production company Shine Group, publicly rebutted an earlier comment by her brother James Murdoch, Deputy Chief Operating Officer of News Corporation, in reference to the British Broadcasting Commission, that: "The only reliable, durable and perpetual guarantor of independence is profit," with the observation that: "profit without purpose is a recipe for disaster. Profit must be our servant, not our master." (James MacTaggart Memorial Lecture, Edinburgh Television Festival 2012, available at: www.guardian.co.uk/media/interactive/2012/aug/23/elisabeth-murdoch-mactaggart-lecture.)

9 See, for example, www.caradvice.com.au/55225/toyota-ceo-deeply-sorry-for-worldwide-pedal-recall/

10 Parts of this Framework were presented in Dransfield, Fisher and Vogel (1999).

4   What is Stakeholder Value?

4.1   INTRODUCTION

> **Value**. That amount of some commodity, medium of exchange,
> etc., which is considered to be an equivalent for something else;
> a fair or adequate equivalent or return.
>
> *Oxford English Dictionary*

In the mid-1980s, AT&T was confronted by a paradox:[1] on the one
hand, customer satisfaction levels were running at about 95 percent;
on the other hand, they lost 6 percent market share, where 1 percent
was worth $600,000,000. For the first time in corporate history,
AT&T laid people off – 25,000 worldwide from an overall staff of
300,000 – including managers recently rewarded for the apparently
outstanding customer satisfaction performance.

An AT&T trouble-shooting team discovered that one of the
critical factors explaining the paradox was the way in which
customer satisfaction was being measured: AT&T's overall focus
was not concentrated on their customers' perceptions of Value. And
it turned out to be Value that had a connection to business results.

The concept of creating and adding Value for stakeholders is at
the core of our approach to performance measurement. No matter
which stakeholder group we choose, the question is always the same:

What does Value mean to them?

And as we've seen in Chapter 3, just asking this simple question leads
immediately to issues of market segmentation, regardless of the type
of stakeholder.

The word "Value" obviously connotes some sort of exchange or
trade: you get something you want, you give something in return.

Once we've decided the nature of this exchange, at least at a very basic level, we're then faced with further questions:

- Why bother with Value? How do we know that it has any relationship to our business?
- What sorts of things can we work on to increase Value?

We'll look at these two issues in general terms before we start focusing on particular groups of stakeholders.

4.2   CONNECTING VALUE TO BUSINESS PERFORMANCE

First, we need to distinguish between

> *Value*

and

> *Value Added*, or *Relative Value*

Ideally, you want to be able to measure *Value Added*. This is the additional Value your enterprise adds for a stakeholder group relative to what they can get from the competition. As we'll see, *Value Added*, or *Relative Value*, is critical in delivering superior business performance, especially in the Customer market.

However, it can be very difficult to obtain the data needed to calculate *Relative Value*, in which case, you need to fall back on surrogate metrics to allow you to calibrate the Value you are providing. This can be done in various ways.

One approach is to identify a connection between Value (a perceptual, or "soft," metric) and a hard ("accounting") metric, *e.g.*

- between Customer Value and Market Share
- between People Value and staff turnover
- between Partner Value and Joint Business Profitability
- between Community Value and Commercialization Outcomes.

Another approach is to connect Stakeholder Value to some sort of measure of loyalty. What sorts of responses do you want to elicit from your stakeholders in response to superior performance by your enterprise? Some desirable reactions include:

From your Customers
- Willingness to repurchase
- Willingness to recommend your products or services to others.

From People working in your enterprise
- Willingness to recommend you as an employer
- A place where they can do their best work.

From your Partners
- Willingness to work with you on other projects
- Willingness to recommend to other enterprises as someone to supply, or with whom to co-venture.

From the Community
- Willingness to support your presence in the area
- Willingness to support your enterprise by purchasing your products and services.

From your Owners/Shareholders
- Willingness to invest in your enterprise
- Willingness to recommend investment to others.

The connection tends to take the form of a Value–Loyalty graph devised by Ray Kordupleski, which relates the Value score (on a scale of 1 to 10, where 1 = Poor and 10 = Excellent) to the percentage of your target stakeholder group providing a high rating on one of these metrics. Exhibit 4.1 shows the typical appearance of such a graph, and how it can be used both to assess the current Value score, and select a target for the next period.

These graphs can be calculated from data obtained when Value surveys are conducted.

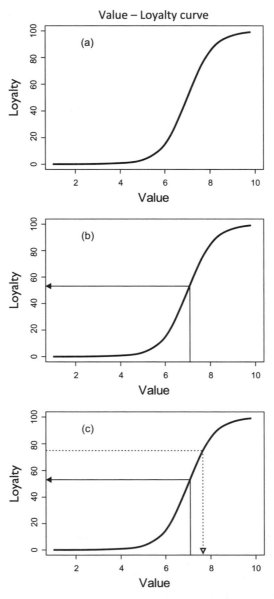

EXHIBIT 4.1. (a) A Value–Loyalty graph shows the typical relationship between Value, on a 10-point scale, and the percentage of people who are very willing to show some form of Loyalty, such as being very willing to recommend your enterprise to others; (b) In this example, the specific score Value = 7.1 corresponds to about 63 % of people being very willing to recommend; (c) If the 12-month target for Loyalty is chosen as 75%, this means that the Value score has to be increased to about 7.65.

EXHIBIT 4.2. The same basic cyclic process is used for creating and adding Value, for each stakeholder.

The Stakeholder Value Improvement Cycle

1. Understand what Value means to a stakeholder, and identify the key drivers of Value, and how to connect Value to higher-level business drivers.
2. Put measures and measurement processes in place to acquire data.
3. Acquire and analyze Value survey data.
4. Identify the improvement priorities that will have the greatest impact on Value, *and hence on your business.*
5. Make the improvements and communicate the improvements to the stakeholder.
   Go to (3).

So that's why we focus on Value: it can be connected to higher-level business drivers. Now for the second issue: *What sorts of things can we work on to increase Value?*

In the next few chapters, we'll look at a way of creating and improving Stakeholder Value that has two important properties:

- It provides your leadership team with a means of selecting improvement priorities, by identifying what you can work on that is likely to have the biggest impact on Stakeholder Value and, hence, through Value–Loyalty and other connections, on your business bottom line.
- It helps align people and systems with the purpose of the enterprise.

We can use the same process for each stakeholder group (see Exhibit 4.2).

We start with creating and adding Value for Customers, because that was the original context for developing the process.

NOTE

1 This is recounted in detail in Kordupleski (2003).

5   Adding Value for Customers

Do not pursue money. He who pursues money will never achieve it.
Serve! If you serve as best you can, you will not be able to escape money.

Tomas Bata[1]

The concept of "assets" is also changing. Profitability and growth today
come from the skilful management of many assets, a great many of which
are not reflected in the accountant's view of the balance sheet, and are
intangible. Customer relationships are the most crucial of these assets.
The competition for customers and customer bases is becoming fierce.
Management focus must shift towards management of this critical asset.

Richard Normann[2]

PART I   CUSTOMER VALUE AND BUSINESS IMPACT

Why are you losing market share? Which competitors represent the
biggest threats? Why are customers only purchasing once? Do you
really understand the Value Proposition you are presenting to the
market? Where should you focus effort to develop competitive advantage, and what sort of effort will it take?

This chapter shows you a way to respond to all of these
questions. The bottom line is: if your customers perceive that they
get more *Value* from your enterprise than from elsewhere, they'll stay
with you, and they'll recommend you to others. That represents
success in the marketplace.

5.1   WHAT IS VALUE FOR CUSTOMERS?

One of W. Edwards Deming's most quoted aphorisms was: "Why ask
the customer what he wants? How would he know?" As is often the
case with such advice, it provides good guidance in many situations,
but rogue counter-examples will deny it its place as a universal verity.
The late Steve Jobs served as a rogue in this instance, delighting

people with products and services they didn't realize they wanted, until they appeared – not dissimilar to the Sony Walkman story, but even more spectacularly successful. Jobs proved, time after time, that if you delight customers with a premium product, you can charge a premium price.[3] In other words, it's all about Value.

The simplest expression of Value for Customers is:

Is this product or service worth what I paid for it?

in other words, their satisfaction with the *Quality* of what they received, balanced against the *Price* they had to pay for it.

Over time, a third factor has been emerging as having strong direct influence on the overall assessment of Value: the *Image* of your company. Of course, this has long been recognized for iconic brands like IBM (*"Nobody ever got fired for buying IBM equipment"*), Rolls-Royce and Rolex, but it is a far more widespread effect because of the veritable blizzard of advertising material in today's marketplaces.

Value and its three drivers provide us with the top level of a so-called Customer Value tree as shown in Exhibit 5.1.

Have things been over-simplified? Exhibit 5.2 poses three critical questions.

To answer questions B and C, we need to describe the key steps involved in managing Customer Value. Then we'll apply the same steps for all other stakeholders. First, though, let's look at the connection between Customer Value and business results, from which it emerges that what really matters is *Value relative to the competition*.

Ray Kordupleski, the lead developer of the Customer Value methodology that we'll be using, has studied this issue extensively[4]

Quality

Worth What
Paid For

Image

Price

EXHIBIT 5.1. Value and its drivers for Customers. The concept of Value is captured by the term Worth What Paid For.

EXHIBIT 5.2. Three important questions about Customer Value.

A. How do we know that Customer Value is important to the business?
B. How do we know that Quality, Image and Price are the only important drivers of Value, and that there isn't some other big factor?
C. Where are the numbers coming from, and how do we use them?

through a wide range of case studies by looking for direct links between Customer Value and (in his words):

- Market Share (winning customers)
- Share of wallet (keeping customers and increasing the amount of business they do with you)
- Return on Invested Capital (satisfying shareholders).

His book contains compelling evidence that the critical high-level customer metric[5] is *Customer Value Added*, or *CVA*:

$$CVA = \frac{Perceived\ worth\ of\ your\ offer}{Perceived\ worth\ of\ competitors'\ offers}$$

or, more simply,

$$CVA = \frac{Value\ score\ for\ your\ enterprise}{Value\ score\ for\ competitors}$$

A fine example of the efficacy of this metric derives from an ongoing AT&T Customer Satisfaction program for the Business Telephone Equipment market.

Exhibit 5.3(a) shows two time series for data collected over a few years, the darker curve being AT&T's share of the telephone equipment market (% *installs*) and the lighter curve being the CVA score.

The two curves look very similar. However, there is something not quite correct about this graph. The CVA curve should actually be shifted four months to the left, as in Exhibit 5.3(b). *This suggests that CVA is an important lead indicator for market share.*

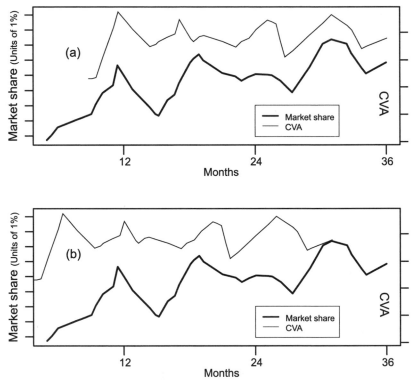

EXHIBIT 5.3. Relating CVA to market share: (a) The time series for market share in AT&T's Business Telephone Equipment market and the time series for the CVA scores appear very similar in shape; (b) In fact, the CVA time series should actually be plotted earlier, indicating that CVA is a good indicator of market share.

In short, after eighteen months of using the customer value data correctly, the CVA score rose 7 points, from 99 to 106, and three months later, market share rose 7 percent.

The lead time need not be anywhere near so long. A benchmarking study by Federal Express revealed changes in market shares within forty-eight hours of changes in their internal metrics.[6]

So far, we've discussed an important issue raised in Section 4.1: *How do we know that (Customer) Value is important to the business?*

Now we turn to the next important issue, in essence: *How do we increase Customer Value, and Customer Value Added?*

PART II   MANAGING CUSTOMER VALUE

5.2   MANAGING VALUE FOR CUSTOMERS: WHERE DOES IT BEGIN?

Exhibit 5.1 showed the top level of a Customer Value tree. Now we can elaborate the branches of the tree, by thinking through the Customer experience *from the Customer's point of view*. A generic example is depicted in Exhibit 5.4.

What's important here?

- There is a clear link between Value (Worth What Paid For) and the main business process delivering the product or service. Improving the Delivery Process will be important in improving Quality.

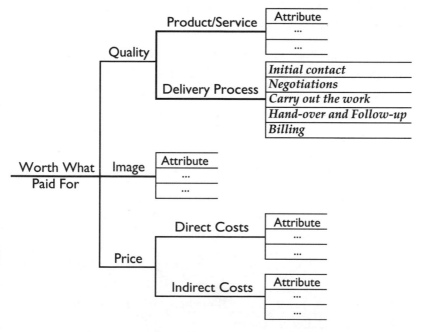

EXHIBIT 5.4. Typical structure of a Customer Value tree. Quality is represented as the Product or Service Received, and the Delivery Process comprising the sequence of Customer experiences in receiving this Product or Service. Price has as its Drivers both Direct Costs and Indirect Costs (or Cost of Doing Business). Each of P/S, DP, Image, DC and IC has a small set of Attributes that are identified from market Focus Groups as the most important quality characteristics of the Driver.

- The customer survey will focus only on the most important factors affecting overall satisfaction. You want a few priorities to work on (the most important ones), not a hundred.
- As we'll see, a huge benefit of this approach is that there's a way of checking whether something important has been omitted.
- There is a clear structure associated with what we're going to measure.

Why does the structure of the measures matter?

It implies that different sorts of measures are needed in different parts of the performance measurement structure (Exhibit 3.5). And it also implies that you need to know which factors influence which other factors, so that you can focus your improvement efforts where they are likely to result in the biggest increase in Value.

The Customer Value tree forms the basis of a survey of the market. Respondents (decision-makers in their enterprises) are asked to rate the performance of their supplier (you or a competitor) on each Attribute, then on the higher-level driver, and so on all the way up to Value. Ratings are on a 10-point scale, where 1 = Poor and 10 = Excellent.

The real power of this approach becomes apparent when the data are analyzed statistically.

Firstly, you can check that nothing important is missing from the survey. Statistical analysis will confirm whether:

- the ratings for Value are well-predicted by those for Quality, Image and Price
- the ratings for Quality are well-predicted by those for Product/ Service and Delivery Process
- the ratings for Product/Service are well-predicted by those for its Attributes, *etc.*

Secondly, you can identify where to focus your improvement priorities. The results will tell you:

EXHIBIT 5.5. A top-level Customer Value competitive profile. Your overall Value score is 7.3, compared with your competition which averages 7.5, so your CVA score is below par at 97 percent. (Par would be a CVA score in the range 98–102, allowing for the variability in the data.) The ratings are on a 10-point scale, where 1 = Poor and 10 = Excellent.

Driver	Impact weight (%)	Mean rating (precision ± 0.10)*		Relative rating (%)
		Your company	Competition	
Quality (Q)	42	7.7	7.6	101
Image (I)	15	7.1	7.3	97
Price (P)	30	6.9	7.0	98
Value (V)		7.3	7.5	97

*Note: A precision of ± 0.10 means (for example) that 7.7 ± 0.10 is a 95 percent confidence interval for the mean Quality rating for your company.

- the relative importance of all these drivers and Attributes in terms of influencing Value; and
- how you are rated relative to the competition.

And that's just what you need to help you select your priorities for improvement: something that helps you focus on important factors (high Impact weight) where you are rated poorly. Exhibit 5.5 shows a typical top-level summary of the situation.

In this table, focus on two columns: the **Impact weight** column, which indicates the relative importance of Quality, Image and Price in terms of explaining the overall rating of Value; and the **Relative rating** column at the right hand side, that shows your rating compared with the average of your competitors. A range[7] of 98–102 for the relative rating denotes a par score (no detectable difference between you and the average of your competitors).

What are the key messages in this table?

- Overall, the market perceives you as performing just below par (V_{you} = 7.3) compared with the average of your competitors (V_{comp} = 7.5).

- The perception of Quality is the most important factor (Impact weight 42 percent) driving the rating for Value. You are at par here.
- You have identified the most important drivers of Value. The Impact weights add to 87 percent, so the totality of other factors accounts for only 13 percent. You can act with confidence on these results.

How should you proceed? Start by choosing a target for improvement in your Value score, then identify the specific improvements.

5.3   CHOOSING A TARGET VALUE SCORE

There are a couple of ways to explore this. The first is to look at your position on a Value Map.[8] Exhibit 5.6 shows the basic elements of a Value Map, on which your Value position, in terms of your relative scores on Quality and Price, is to be plotted against the competition.

With the results you have obtained, the Value Maps looks like Exhibit 5.7.

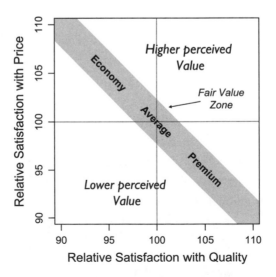

EXHIBIT 5.6. Prototype of a Value Map. Scores for Relative Quality and Relative Price are plotted against those of the competitors. The Fair Value zone relates to which market sector you are targeting.

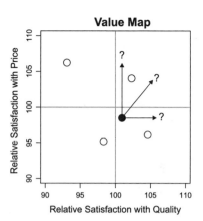

EXHIBIT 5.7. Value Maps. The score for enterprise is shown as the solid dot in graph (a). There is no market leader, although there are clear leaders on Quality and on Price. The three arrows in graph (b) show three possible strategies, depending on whether you want to compete on Quality, on Price, or on both.

Do you want to compete on Quality or on Price, or on both? This depends on where you want to position yourself in the market.

You can also look at your Value–Loyalty graphs. For example, for the Loyalty metric *percentage of customers very willing to repurchase*, your graph might look like Exhibit 5.8 for these data. Your current Value score of 7.3 corresponds to about 63 percent of your Customers being very willing to repurchase from you. That's not surprising, given where you're sitting on the Value Map. There are competitors who are better on Quality and on Price. What will be your twelve-month goal for Customer Loyalty? Seventy-five percent? Exhibit 5.8 indicates that you need to achieve a Value score of at least 7.8. How will you make the improvements to achieve this?

You can direct your company's efforts to those areas that have high impact on *Value* and are rated poorly – *relative to the competition*. You're not the only person in the market gathering customer data. Your competitors are out there doing the same thing. *And what is critical is that you are perceived as delivering superior Value,*

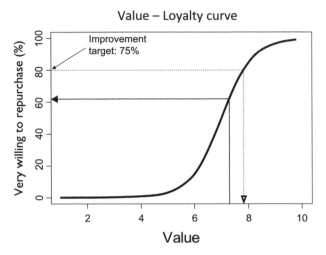

EXHIBIT 5.8. Deciding on an improvement goal based on the Value–Loyalty curve. The current Value rating of 7.3 corresponds to just 63% of your customers being very willing to repurchase from you. If you want this to be at least 80% within 12 months, you'll need to raise your Value score to about 7.8.

which will derive from superior performance on high Impact factors further down the tree.

Indeed, one of the lower-level metrics may appear temporarily in the regular Board and Leadership reports, because of its critical importance to improving your competitive position. This is one of the reasons for describing the whole process – so you can see where some of the metrics originate.

5.4   SELECTING YOUR IMPROVEMENT PRIORITIES

Pricing in the service business is less influenced by cost than it is by the customer's perception of "value" or "worth."

Richard Normann[9]

Start by revisiting the results in Exhibit 5.5, and the comments that go with it. We've just seen that there are various possible strategies, depending on how you want to compete – improving relative Quality, improving relative Price, or both. The goal is to achieve an improvement in Value to 7.8, 0.5 above where you are now. How might this be achievable?

It probably needs three improvement teams, one focusing on Quality, one on Image, and one on Price. Suppose you set them the following stretch targets:

- improve Quality (Q) by 0.5 (7.7 → 8.2)
- improve Image (I) by 0.7 (7.1 → 7.8)
- improve Price (P) by 0.6 (6.9 → 7.5).

Based on the Impact weights in Exhibit 5.5, that will get you a predicted improvement of:

$$0.42 \times \text{Increase in Q} + 0.15 \times \text{Increase in I} + 0.30 \times \text{Increase in P}$$
$$= 0.42 \times 0.5 + 0.15 \times 0.7 + 0.30 \times 0.6$$
$$= 0.495$$

which is very close to your goal of 0.5.

Now your improvement teams can swing into action, using whatever improvement technology your company utilizes (Six Sigma, or something else). They are working with lower-level tables. For example, the Quality team may have Exhibits 5.9 and 5.10 in front of them, relating to a Product you produce:

EXHIBIT 5.9. Competitive profile for the two drivers of Quality. Your company's product is perceived as quite superior to those of your competitors. However, the Delivery Process has more than double the impact on the market's perception of overall Quality, and here your performance is significantly below par.

Driver	Impact weight (%)	Mean rating (precision ± 0.10)		Relative rating (%)
		Your company	Competition	
Product	30	8.5	7.9	107
Delivery Process	62	7.1	7.5	95
Quality		7.7	7.6	101

EXHIBIT 5.10. Competitive profile for the sub-processes in the Delivery Process. Your company appears to be very good at winning contracts but nowhere near as good while the work is being done, or when handing over or billing.

Driver	Impact weight (%)	Mean rating (precision ± 0.10)		Relative rating (%)
		Your company	Competition	
Initial contact	13	7.8	7.5	104
Negotiation	15	7.7	7.2	106
Carry out work	19	7.1	7.8	91
Handover and follow-up	23	6.9	7.6	91
Billing	21	6.4	7.4	87
Delivery Process		7.1	7.5	95

Exhibit 5.9 suggests that your company makes products preferred by the market, but that their experience in dealing with you has a far greater influence on their overall view of Quality. So you need to concentrate on improving the Delivery Process.

The improvement team working on this aspect (which should include a representative from each of the departments involved) will observe, in Exhibit 5.10, that your sales force and legal group are working well to secure contracts. However, once they've won the business, the customer's experience goes downhill. The team would now explore what's happening in some detail, reviewing customer complaints, identifying the key customer requirements for each, and commissioning a Transaction survey[10] to identify the root causes of customer dissatisfaction. This is where you can put in place *operational metrics* to track customer requirements such as *Responsiveness, Promises Kept, Knowledgeable people, etc.*[11]

For example, some of the root causes may well relate to how telephone queries and complaints are handled – being bounced around from one department to another, not calling back as promised, and so on. Your performance here can be tracked using metrics such as *percentage of enquiries handled on first call*. Someone needs to be accountable for improving this metric, which may even appear in Leadership reports as a time series graph, until such time as the relevant ratings improve to their target values.

The schematic in Exhibit 5.11 summarizes the measurement phase.

And so the team identifies the target improvement in each rating, puts metrics like this in place, and sets about improving the business. In Ray Kordupleski's language:[12]

Choose Value (focus your priorities)
    → Deliver Value (manage your business processes)
        → Communicate Value (educate the market)

5.5   COMPETING IN RAPIDLY CHANGING MARKETS

Are you competing in a market where change is occurring rapidly, whether it be changing market tastes or rapid emergence of new products or product features, or media-driven fads?

Or do you want to make a rapid assessment of an initiative you have just launched, or a counter to bad publicity?

In such situations, you may not be able to afford to wait for four- or six-monthly survey results to become available. It is possible to acquire Customer Value survey data on a daily basis, and to analyze it to produce time series of changing impact weights and ratings. We'll see an example of this in the next chapter, on managing People Value, where being in touch with sudden mood changes in the whole enterprise can make the difference between making a timely response to turn things around, and losing some of your best people.

5.6   MANAGING KEY ACCOUNTS

Some markets are totally unsuited to telephone or web-based surveys. You may have a client who is so large or so important to your business as to deserve personal treatment. A special process, *Key Account*

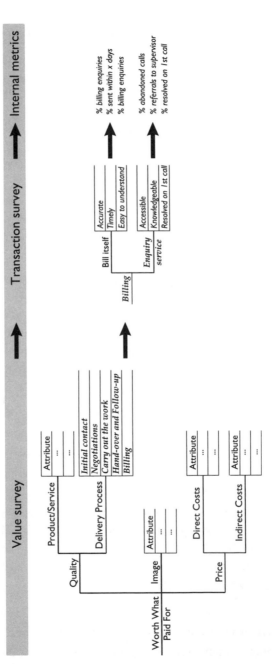

EXHIBIT 5.11. Complete chain of actions for development of internal metrics. Priorities identified in a Value survey trigger a Transaction survey for an important business process, leading to identification of Operational quality attributes and internal metrics that can be tracked to monitor improvement. Based on a diagram developed by Ray Kordupleski.

Value Management, provides a powerful means of monitoring and improving the relationship.

The process is best carried out by an external facilitator. Once you know that the client is willing to participate, the main steps are:

1. The facilitator holds a meeting with your management team for this Key Account, to develop *your best guess* at the client's Value tree, and to identify people to interview – the client's decision-maker and key influencers.
2. A program of interviews is established, about ninety minutes for each of the most senior officers, and sixty minutes with the others.
3. In each interview, the facilitator builds those parts of the tree with which the interviewee is familiar, obtains both impact weights and ratings for these parts and, if possible, obtains competitive ratings – how the interviewee views your competitors. For summary ratings (Value, Quality, Price, Image, Product/Service) and for particularly high or low ratings, ask for the reason.
4. The interviewer then compiles a summary Value tree together with a synthesized set of comments, and feeds this back to the Key Account management team in a planning workshop.
5. A copy of the report is then supplied to the client of the Key Account, together with the planned responses.
6. Subsequent updates to the scores can be done by telephone interview.

One powerful aspect of this approach is that clients will sometimes provide candid comments to the facilitator to be reported back to you that they won't make to you directly. Another is the potential to reveal significant dislocation in communication channels, even in the client's organization.

For example, in conducting this process with two different clients on behalf of a major supplier of R&D services, the following occurred:

• One large mineral exploration company, in comparing the R&D provider with their competitors, observed that whereas their competitors spent a large amount of time on site in remote terrain, "treating our site as their laboratory," the R&D provider "had thick veils of cobwebs between their office and the airport."

- Another mineral processing company had its own in-house R&D laboratory that nonetheless sub-contracted specific R&D projects to the R&D provider. When the Chief Financial Officer was interviewed, he assigned 100 percent of the impact weight to Price and none to Quality or Image, and then gave Price a very low rating and said that he wanted to halve the level of contracted research. When asked why, he said that he was totally unaware of any of the benefits of the research being provided, as the head of his R&D laboratory had never bothered to explain them. He thought it was largely a waste of money.

This process for managing Key Accounts is, in fact, the primary approach to managing Value for Partnerships, as we'll see shortly.

5.7   WHAT IS A VALUE PROPOSITION?

You've often heard the term, but have you ever heard anyone define what they really meant when they used it? The Customer Value competitive profiles allow you to be very specific, when you devise a "Value Proposition" for a market.

Start with Exhibit 5.5 and Exhibit 5.7. What position have you selected on the Value Map? One possible strategy is:

- Market leader on Quality
- Market leader on Image
- At par on Price.

Then move down through the competitive profiles and set your target ratings to deliver these high-level results. That's your Value Proposition.

5.8   CODA: FINAL COMMENT ON SHARED VALUE

The discussion in this chapter has, by and large, been aligned with a traditional Customer–Supplier paradigm. However, times and paradigms change. In a discussion of Value chains, Normann and Ramirez remark[13]

Economic actors no longer relate to each other in the simple, unidirectional, sequential arrangement described by the value chain notion. The relationship between any two actors tends to be far more complex than can be conceptually captured by the unidirectional "make/buy" model underlining the value chain. Instead of "adding" value one after the other, the partners in the production of an offering create value together through varied types of "co-productive" relationships.[14]

In a simpler situation, changes have been discussed by Bertini and Gourville, where they observe that[15]

Traditional pricing strategy is by definition antagonistic, but it needs to become a more socially conscious, collaborative exercise. Business should ... recognize that humanizing the way they generate revenue can open up opportunities to create additional value. That means viewing customers as partners in value creation – a collaboration that increases customers' engagement and taps their insights about the value they seek and how firms can deliver it. The result is a bigger pie, which benefits firms and customers alike.

In short, in their language, focus on relationships, not on transactions.

At a more strategic level, the Customer–Supplier relationship may move to more of a partnership view of co-production of Value, as discussed in Chapter 7.

NOTES

1 Quoted in Rybka (2008).
2 Normann (2001) page 19.
3 A few weeks after Steve Jobs' death, Baggini (2011) published an article on how Jobs had changed capitalism, in which he wrote:

"Take the old adage that the consumer is king. In some ways, this is as true for Apple as it is for anyone else. It stands or falls on the basis of whether people will buy its stuff. But Jobs's success was built firmly on the idea that in another sense, you should not give consumers what they want because they don't know what they want. No one thought they wanted the first desktop Mac, iPod, iPhone or iPad before they existed. Jobs repeatedly created things that people came to want more than anything else only by not trying to give them what they already wanted. This challenges the idea that consumer culture inevitably means pandering to the conventional, to the lowest common denominator. Markets are not necessarily conservative: truly great innovations can become popular.

"Jobs has also provided the clearest evidence yet that excellence comes at a cost. Against both the optimistic open-source movement that thinks all good things can be made collaboratively for free, and the race-to-the-bottom chains that believe the answer is always to be the cheapest, Jobs showed that you could, and must, charge a premium price for a premium product. Far from condemning his company to a niche, by following this principle, Apple actually became, briefly, the biggest company in the world. The lesson has still to be taken on board elsewhere. In news and broadcasting, for example, we are all learning that you can't sustain quality by giving things away.

"It's not just about cost, however. Jobs was unpopular for the way in which he tightly controlled Apple's copyrights, refused to license to third parties and tied his devices to his own suppliers of content. This was seen as undemocratic, demagogic even. But whether or not he was always right, his success shows that there is something to the idea that true excellence often requires tight control. It's the principle that guides the best restaurant kitchens, the best production lines and even many of the best films, plays or dance productions. Jobs should have killed the idea that everything works better if it's open, collaborative and non-judgmental."
©Julian Baggini/The Guardian 2013.

4 Kordupleski (2003), page 6 *et seq.*
5 However, improving this overall Customer-focused metric will depend on improving several lower-level metrics. Some people have advocated the so-called *Net Promoter Score* (NPS) as the only customer loyalty metric needed to manage the Customer (or, for that matter, its analog for People or for any other major stakeholder group); see *e.g.* Reichheld (2003) for the original suggestion. NPS is derived by asking customers a single question – "How likely is it that you would recommend our company to a friend or colleague?" – with responses recorded on an 11-point scale (0–10), where 0 means *Not at all likely* and 10 means *Extremely likely*. Respondents are

then classified as Detractors (0–6), Passives (7–8) or Promoters (9–10), whence NPS = %(Promoters) − %(Detractors). Whilst it is not a bad metric for measuring Loyalty, it cannot possibly be a helpful metric for management and improvement:

- As an outcome measure, and one that depends to a significant extent on what your competitors are doing, NPS cannot be used for management purposes (a point made more generally elsewhere in this book).
- It focuses only on a subset of the market (one's own customers), and even then, ignores part of that market (the Passives), so is likely to lead to lost market share.
- It is easily manipulated: you simply let go of dissatisfied customers, rather than improving those aspects of your offering that are causing the dissatisfaction!
- Most importantly, NPS is only describing the current situation with regard to the loyalty of current customers. It provides no guidance whatsoever about the factors that create value for the customers and so produce loyalty, and hence no guidance about what the enterprise needs to work on to retain existing customers and gain new ones. And such guidance will require collecting data on several Drivers and Attributes of Value. It cannot be gained from a single number. Would you attempt to manage the financial aspect of your business by focusing on a single metric, such as *Profit*?

6 Kordupleski (2003), page 9.
7 *i.e.* a 95 percent confidence interval.
8 Kordupleski (2003), page 25 *et seq.*
9 Normann (2001), page 126.
10 Kordupleski (2003), pages 25, 131 *et seq.*
11 In a fine piece of observational research, Ray Kordupleski (*ibid.*, page 249) has identified nine basic quality attributes that, however expressed, tend to cover the customer requirements for any service process. These are:

- Accessibility
- Responsiveness
- Knowledgeable people
- Promptness
- Promises kept
- Kept informed

- Follow-up
- No surprises
- Do it the right way the first time.

12 Kordupleski (2003), page 241.
13 Normann and Ramirez (1994), page 29.
14 Normann and Ramirez's footnote on the same page is worth reading. In essence, it points out that the traditional Value chain concept is not irrelevant to today's business; rather, it is just a somewhat limited view.
15 Bertini and Gourville (2012), building on earlier work by Porter and Kramer (2011).

6   Adding Value for People

We advertised for staff and people came along.

Anita Roddick[1]

I believe the real difference between success and failure in a corporation can very often be traced to the question of how well the organization brings out the great energies and talents of its people.

Thomas J. Watson, Jr.

PART I   PEOPLE VALUE AND BUSINESS IMPACT

6.1   PREAMBLE: WHY BOTHER?

How much of your budget is spent on remunerating your people: salary, bonuses, provision for retirement *etc.*? 10 million dollars? 100 million dollars? More?

Would you like to save yourself at least 0.5 percent to 1 percent of this annually? There is a simple solution: cut your *unplanned staff turnover* by 1 percent.

It is very costly to lose someone you hadn't wanted to lose. You lose money through:

- recruitment processes
- downtime pending appointment
- cost of load sharing
- cost of new hire
- time to become proficient.

For lower-level staff, staff loss is generally reckoned to cost of the order of 50 percent of their total annual package, rising to 100 percent *or more* for senior people. And we haven't even started to add in the cost of the knowledge and know-how that walked out the door.

Some enterprises have very low staff turnover – for example, universities and other R&D organizations where many of the staff spend a lifetime building their research careers. Others, such as building and construction companies, can easily run at 15–20 percent unplanned staff turnover. And a leading events management company runs at 45 percent. There's a lot of money to be saved.

Quite apart from the direct impact on the bottom line, there is a wealth of informal evidence for what might be termed the Sears Value Chain, as Sears' research ascertained more than a decade ago:[2]

Superior value for people
   → Superior value for customers
      → Superior value for the business

There is also a wealth of argument, from the early research by Douglas McGregor[3] to recent studies by Dave Ulrich and Norm Smallwood,[4] about the importance and value of people's discretionary effort in improving business performance. More generally, Jac Fitz-Enz has been arguing the case for effective use of "human capital" metrics and analytics since 1978.[5]

In the same way that you manage Value for your Customers, you can manage Value for your People. And we're not talking about just running an annual staff survey. How would you like to receive information about your financials once a year, rather than once a month or once a quarter? That is, of course, ridiculous. You can't "manage" anything with such infrequent data. All you can do is wring your hands at the bad news that has arrived months too late for timely intervention.

In describing Customer Value surveys, we provided broad justification for their structure, and also looked at some more general reasons for carrying out Customer Satisfaction surveys, and what this implied for construction of surveys.

Not surprisingly, you can – *and should* – ask the same sorts of questions about other stakeholder satisfaction surveys. If you're not clear about what you really need from these surveys, they'll end up poorly designed, waste your money, and probably annoy the stakeholder, who won't see much benefit from responding to them. Exhibit 6.1 provides some of the key reasons for carrying out People Value surveys, and what this means for how they are designed.

Since the process for managing People Value is just like the corresponding process for Customers, we'll basically just look at the differences. However, there is one particular aspect that we will describe in detail that wasn't covered in the previous chapter: using continuous monitoring surveys. This can be really powerful stuff, as we'll see in a case study.

EXHIBIT 6.1. Some reasons for carrying out staff surveys and their implications for survey design. With slight modification, they are applicable to any sort of stakeholder survey.

Why carry out staff surveys?

- Find out what's important to people when they decide where to work.
- Ascertain what your organization's Image is like, as an employer.
- Obtain timely feedback.
- Find out what you need to fix, and with what priority.
- Detect changes in the market – *e.g.* changing work styles and life styles.
- Find out how the competition is viewed.
- Ultimately, improve your business bottom line!

What does this imply about survey design?

- Ask the right questions.
- Find a way of benchmarking the results.
- Survey sufficiently often that you get timely data.
- Ensure that the resulting data are actionable.
- Make the survey user-friendly – not too long or complex – in order to get a reasonable response rate and accurate responses.
- Provide links to higher-level business drivers.

6.2 WHAT IS VALUE FOR PEOPLE?

The beatings will continue until morale improves.

W. Edwards Deming

What does Value *mean for People?*

It will be captured with a question: *All things considered, is it worth working here?* and represented in terms of three principal drivers:

- the *Work* people do,
- the *Image* of your enterprise, and
- the *Remuneration* they receive for doing their job,

which define the highest level of a People Value tree, as shown in Exhibit 6.2.

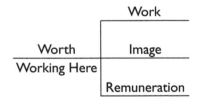

EXHIBIT 6.2. Value and its drivers for People. The concept of Value is captured by the term Worth Working Here.

We'll see more detail about this tree shortly. First, we need to see how People Value might have an impact on your business bottom line, by connecting it to other high-level business drivers.

6.3 LINKING PEOPLE VALUE TO CUSTOMER VALUE AND BUSINESS PERFORMANCE

There are a number of ways to connect an overall People Value score to higher-level business drivers and to Customer Value. For example:

- Using Value–Loyalty graphs similar to Exhibit 4.1. Possible things to measure on the Loyalty axis would include:
  - Willingness to recommend your enterprise as a place to work.
  - Extent to which your employees are able to do their best work.

And, of course, people's ability to do their best work relates to their willingness to put in extra – *i.e. discretionary* – effort, which we noted earlier as an important driver of business success.

- Cross-correlating *People Value* with *staff turnover* over time, by analogy with Exhibit 5.3
- Cross-correlating *People Value* with *Customer Value* over time, by analogy with Exhibit 5.3
- At a lower level, cross-correlating relevant attributes in the *People Value* tree to important attributes in the *Customer Value* tree.[6]

In contrast with Customer Value surveys, it is very difficult to get competitive data for People Value surveys, as this would require surveying people who work for your competitors and who would have no interest in assisting you. A more likely approach is to arrange a benchmarking agreement with enterprises that are in similar but non-competitive industries. Benchmark on the drivers marked in bold in Exhibit 6.3.

PART II   MANAGING PEOPLE VALUE

6.4   MANAGING PEOPLE VALUE IN PRACTICE

Just like managing Customer Value, we follow the basic cycle in Exhibit 4.2.

One possible People Value tree that has worked well in case studies is shown in Exhibit 6.3. In this tree, Work is represented in terms of:

- Work Itself: the actual job you do
- Work Environment: the resources, processes, structures and policies provided to support you in doing your job
- Workplace Culture: what it's like to work at your enterprise.

Remuneration appears with two drivers,

- Financial Benefits: direct financial compensation
- Non-financial Benefits: not directly financial compensation to the individual, but otherwise of benefit.

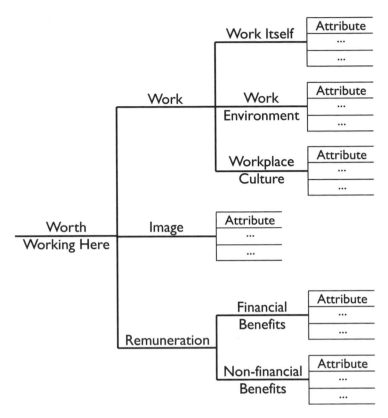

EXHIBIT 6.3. Typical structure of a People Value tree. Quality is represented as the Work is decomposed into three drivers, as is Remuneration. As with Customer Value trees, each driver has a small set of Attributes that are identified from market Focus Groups as the most important quality characteristics of each of these drivers. The drivers printed in bold can be used for benchmarking.

Non-financial Benefits are particularly important in enterprises that have restricted possibilities for increasing salary, bonuses and stock holdings. This is often the case for government and not-for-profit organizations.

The attributes for each of the drivers of Work, Image and Remuneration are chosen to provide a description of a person's "ideal job." Some possible attributes are shown in Exhibit 6.4.

EXHIBIT 6.4. Some typical Attributes in a People Value tree. The aim is to find 6–8 Attributes for each driver that collectively help to define an ideal job if the enterprise performs well on all of them.

Some commonly used Attributes for a People Value tree

Work Itself

- Stimulating work
- Having a clear understanding of my job
- Work that helps me grow and learn
- Work that enables me to maintain a balance between my working life and my personal life.

Work Environment

- Authority to make decisions
- Resources
- Support services
- Training and development
- Supportive systems and structures.

Workplace Culture

- Enterprise committed to workplace safety
- Enterprise has a responsible approach to environmental issues
- People encouraged to work to a common purpose.

Image

- Recognized as a leading company in its area
- Recognized as an employer of choice
- Well-led and well-managed.

Financial Benefits

- Competitive salary
- Bonus and incentive scheme
- My performance linked to my remuneration.

Non-financial Benefits

- Leave provisions
- Flexible working arrangements
- Lifestyle benefits.

The tree in Exhibit 6.3 differs from the Customer Value tree (Exhibit 5.4) in one major respect: there is no direct link between Value and the core business process for managing People Value, which is, of course, the annual performance management cycle. A tree constructed as direct analog to Exhibit 5.4 might look like the one in Exhibit 6.5, the difference being the area in gray. The main reason for not using this is that many organizations simply haven't got such a process sufficiently well embedded in their management systems that people can make sensible assessments.

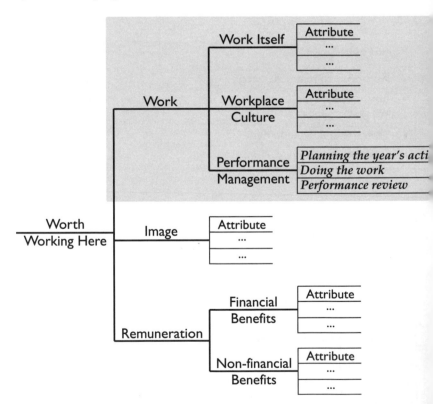

EXHIBIT 6.5. Alternative structure for a People Value tree, with the core business process (performance management) now explicit. The area in gray denotes the difference from the model discussed earlier (Exhibit 6.3).

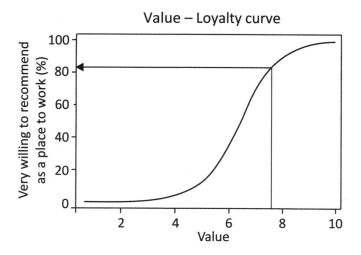

EXHIBIT 6.6. Value–Loyalty graph for an initial People Value survey of staff working on a major infrastructure project. The initial overall Value score of 7.6 corresponded to more than 80 percent of respondents being very willing to recommend the project to others as one to work on.

So now you can run a survey, collect and analyze the data, and take action on the results just as with Customer Value data. Here, you use the People Value–Loyalty graphs as a starting point for setting an improvement goal for People Value.

Exhibit 6.6 shows a Value–Loyalty graph for an initial People Value survey of staff working on a major infrastructure project. The high level of Loyalty indicates strong enthusiasm for the project, an important issue for large engineering projects, which are always competing in a tight market for engineers.

On the basis of the People Value results, the infrastructure project leadership identified six general areas in which to focus improvements (Safety being an ongoing and dominant issue):

1. The performance management system
2. *"My Signature Project"* – a process aimed at communicating the mission and vision for the project (as the best such tunneling

project ever conducted, on certain criteria – Quality of tunneling, cost control, *etc.*) and capturing people's personal goals

3. Other management systems
4. Work/Life balance
5. Salaries
6. Bonus.

The complete survey results were explained to all staff at a series of on-site meetings, together with the Project Leader's planned response to each issue, as shown in Exhibit 6.7. A continuous monitoring Value survey then commenced, and ran for the lifetime of the project.

6.5 CONTINUOUS MONITORING VALUE SURVEYS

Survey data are rarely acquired at an instant of time, especially for surveys based on telephone or printed survey forms, so the results usually represent averaging over a number of weeks.

With the increasing use of web-based survey instruments, it's a simple matter to collect the data on a continuous basis, which means you can look at how things change in time.

This not only has all the benefits of a "static" survey (collecting all the survey data over a short period); it also gives you the benefits of timely warnings about important shifts in stakeholders' perceptions of the performance of your enterprise. We'll see how important this can be by looking at a staff survey monitoring process at a government agency.

The People Value process was launched with an initial two-week survey (preserving the anonymity of respondents). Partial results from the initial survey are shown in Exhibit 6.8. (In this survey, the drivers of Work were Work Itself, Work Environment and Image.) The ratings were not good, and there was clearly scope for a lot of improvement.

Based on these results, which were made available to all staff, the leadership of the agency announced some significant improvement

EXHIBIT 6.7. Leadership response to first People Value survey – major tunneling project.

Leadership response to initial People Value survey

The performance management system (PMS):

- Position description developed to let you know what is expected of you
- Individual performance plan allows you to participate in a fair goal setting process
- Development plan sets out process for you to grow and develop
- Review process lets you discuss how you and your supervisor think you are performing
- PMS is linked to salary and bonus.

"My Signature Project":

- Now been resourced
- Project activities established
- PMS has a role to play
- Leadership working on the next stage of roll-out.

Management systems:

- Not as good as it should have been
- Slow in getting the right resources
- Telco now accept problems at head end
- IT systems training now available.

Work/Life balance:

- Means different things to different people
- Flexibility needed on both sides
- PMS has a role to play
- Communicate your needs
- Construction industry – what's the reality?

Salaries:

- Salary review to take effect from the first pay period in January 2005. Increase adjusted for: Cost Price Index, Industry bandwidth (75th percentile), Skills and experience, PMS Review
- Direct link between performance and salary.

Bonus:

- Approved by Joint Venture Management Committee
- Applies to all
- It will be based on: Project overall performance; Performance of the individual project; Performance of the individual (PMS); Length of service on this project.

EXHIBIT 6.8. Profile for part of the initial People Value survey for a government agency. Impact weights have been normalized to add to 100 percent. Actual unexplained variation was 14 percent.

Driver	Impact weight (%)	Mean rating (precision ± 0.20)
Work Itself	50	5.5
Work Environment	24	5.3
Image	26	5.9
Work		5.5

priorities, including introduction of a proper performance management cycle.

A continuous survey was launched a month later. Every week, a number of staff members were selected at random and invited to participate in the survey. The resulting data stream was analyzed after three months. Exhibit 6.9 shows the changes over time of both the mean ratings and their relative importance.

Two important features stand out:

1. The left hand column of graphs shows that for all three drivers, there is an initial improvement in mean ratings, and then the mean ratings drop again towards the end of the period.
2. The relative importance of the three drivers changes dramatically over time:
   - Work Itself, which started out with a relative impact of 50 percent, has effectively dropped to zero by the end of the period.
   - Work Environment, which had only accounted for about 25 percent of the overall influence on Work at the beginning of the survey period, rose to over 70 percent by the end.
   - Image fluctuated a bit, but basically stayed at the same level.

The changes were caused by the sudden dismissal of the head of the agency in the latter part of the survey period. After this happened, people lost all interest in their jobs, and the overall rating of Work was being driven largely by the unsettled Work Environment.

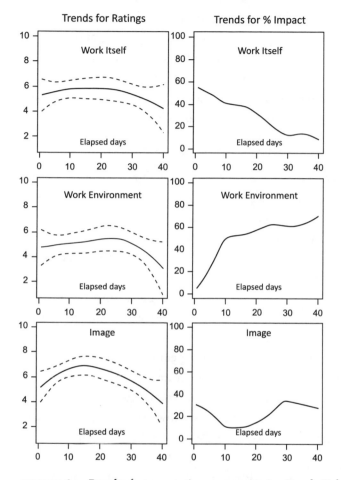

EXHIBIT 6.9. Results from a continuous monitoring People Value survey, over a three-month period. For each of the drivers of Work, the ratings rise initially, then drop away. The corresponding Impact weights for Work Itself and Work Environment change dramatically, with Work Itself losing all its importance, and Work Environment ending up as the dominant influence on Work. This is probably due to the sudden dismissal of the head of the agency, partway through the survey period.

The important point is that this method of surveying can provide timely warning of important changes – in the attitudes of your workforce, in this instance – and so give you the opportunity to intervene before a mass exodus of people occurs.

Exactly the same approach can be used for Customers in fast-moving markets, providing you with the opportunity for timely, possibly pre-emptive, action in response to rapidly changing customer perceptions or requirements. Or it may tell you how well you're managing a disaster, such as having to explain a major product recall and compensate customers for their loss.

6.6   MANAGING VALUE FOR KEY PEOPLE

You may have a few people whom you simply can't afford to lose. So you may want to do something more to manage and improve all aspects of their job than is possible through an anonymous staff survey.

The Key People Value approach is a simple analog of what's done with managing Key Accounts for Customers (Section 5.6). Someone from outside the business unit sits down with each key individual and develops his or her individual People Value tree, complete with ratings, impact weights and comments. This is then fed back to the line manager.

Again, it's an interesting aspect of human behavior that people will be happy for their candid comments to be passed indirectly to their line manager. During one such interview, the individual (a Deputy Director) assigned a very low rating to his satisfaction with Work Itself. When asked for the reason, he said that he saw a number of jobs being given to others that he felt he could do much better. However, he felt unable to speak directly to his line manager about this. In fact, there was a trivial reason for this: the head of the Agency knew perfectly well that he was the best qualified person, but also felt that he was already overburdened. This was rapidly resolved in a brief face-to-face meeting that day and an issue that had been simmering for months was eliminated very quickly.

NOTES

1 Robert Marshall (personal communication), recalling Anita Roddick's presentation to the Australian Quality Conference in Melbourne in 1997.
2 See *e.g.* Rucci, Kirn and Quinn (1998).

3 McGregor (1960)

4 Ulrich and Smallwood (2003).

5 In Fitz-Enz (1978) the author argued for more serious consideration being given to "the use of quantitative data in personnel matters," asserting that "The value and effectiveness of personnel can be measured quantitatively." Many research articles and books later, Fitz-Enz (2013) concluded that: "Measurement (and its sibling, valuation) is the last phase in leveraging human capital. It has often been said that what gets measured gets done. Metrics have three levels: strategic, which is the concern of C-level executives; operational, which is the province of midmanagement; and leading indicators, which help monitor predictive and prescriptive actions. The following are a few of the many metrics and leading indicators companies are using . . ." Most of the metrics recommended by Fitz-Enz in the ensuing list appear in various parts of the system being developed in this book.

6 For example, "Knowledgeable People" is frequently an important attribute of many services processes, in a Customer Value tree. A relevant attribute in the People Value tree would relate to having the training and the resources to do the job properly.

7   Adding Value for Partners

I have found no greater satisfaction than achieving success through
honest dealing and strict adherence to the view that, for you to gain, those
you deal with should gain as well.

Alan Greenspan

If you want to go fast, go alone. If you want to go far, go together.

old African proverb

PART I   PARTNER VALUE AND BUSINESS IMPACT

7.1   WHAT'S A PARTNER?

A. You run a company manufacturing automobile components
    for retail, and your delivery company is becoming
    increasingly unreliable in terms of meeting delivery schedules,
    despite complaints from you and your customers (retail
    outlets) alike.
B. Your company is part of an alliance developing the infrastructure
    to mine a metal deposit. The alliance partner operating the rail link
    to the nearest port is struggling with cash flow.
C. You run a company that manufactures and sells proprietary solar
    cell-based products. You hold some of the key patents, the others
    being held by a software company, with whom you've been
    developing this market-leading technology. Their most important
    patent is now being breached by a competitor, but they cannot
    afford to defend it on their own.

These are all examples of troubled partnerships, but the implications
of the trouble are very different, because the nature of the partnerships
is very different.

The first is a very simple Customer–Supplier partnership. Yes, it
would be best if the delivery company simply fixed things up once the

complaints started; or better still, had anticipated and prevented the loss of control in the first place. However, they haven't met their contractual conditions, and there are plenty of other deliverers wanting business, so you make alternative arrangements at some cost, but you retain your customers and gain peace of mind.

Case (B) is rather more serious. If you don't use a rail link, you have to use road transport, which in this case is much more expensive and much, much less efficient. It may even threaten the viability of this project, although you do have other current projects.

Case (C) is mission-critical. You've been working together on this for years, your planning and budgeting have been done in close collaboration and loss of protection for this patent means loss of your main advantage in the market. Your business and your partner's will live or die together, based on what eventuates.

We can position these three situations on a graph, as shown in Exhibit 7.1.

An important issue to do with partnerships is: *how is Risk shared?* This is not completely straightforward: for example, the vertical axis of Exhibit 7.1, labeled as "Impact," is not necessarily a surrogate for "Sharing of Risk." How this factor is handled needs to be assessed in each of the three models for Partner Value described below.

7.2   PARTNERSHIP VALUE

Not surprisingly, there is considerable variation in the factors driving Value, depending on where the relationship falls in the Partnership space. Exhibit 7.2 shows three different models, ranging from the operational (Customer–Supplier) to the tactical (Alliance – *e.g.* for an infrastructure project) to the strategic (Co-venture, for the long term). Whereas the focus of the first two models is on the quality of the work done, and the remuneration arrangements, the major emphasis of a strategic partnership is on the relationship: the relationship is probably open-ended in duration, so having it work well will be critical to long-term success.

Partnership Value Space

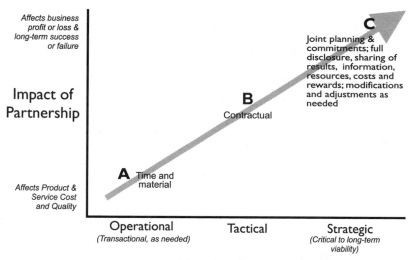

Affects business
profit or loss &
long-term success
or failure

C

Joint planning &
commitments; full
disclosure, sharing of
results, information,
resources, costs and
rewards; modifications
and adjustments as
needed

Impact of
Partnership

B

Contractual

A Time and
material

Affects Product &
Service Cost
and Quality

Operational
(Transactional, as needed)

Tactical

Strategic
(Critical to long-term
viability)

Nature of interaction

EXHIBIT 7.1. There is a continuum of relationships that describe a partnership.[1] However, it is helpful to distinguish three types of partnership, each with a characteristic concept of Value. The characters A, B and C relate to the three partnership scenarios.

Operational model: Suppliers

Worthwhile Customer	Work	~ 45%
	Reputation	~ 10%
	Payment	~ 45%

Tactical model: Alliances

Worthwhile Alliance	Quality of what's done	~ 45%
	Partner's Reputation	~ 10%
	Remuneration arrangements	~ 45%

Strategic model: Co-ventures

Worthwhile Co-venture	Quality of Co-venture	~ 20%
	Quality of Relationship	~ 60%
	Benefits from Relationship	~ 20%

EXHIBIT 7.2. Value means something very different for the different types of partnership. Just as importantly, the relative importance of the three Value drivers in each model reflects the very different nature of each type.

7.3   LINKING PARTNERSHIP VALUE TO BUSINESS PERFORMANCE

This is done just like People Value and Customer Value: you use a Value–Loyalty graph based on expressions of loyalty such as:

- Willingness to partner with you on a new venture
- Willingness to recommend you to others as a Partner.

PART II   MANAGING PARTNER VALUE

7.4   BUILDING THE DIFFERENT PARTNERSHIP MODELS

What is Value for Suppliers?

Exhibit 7.3 shows a simple Value tree model for the most operational form of Partnership, which we call a Supplier relationship. The exhibit also shows some Impact weights for the three principal drivers that are indicative of their likely relative importance when

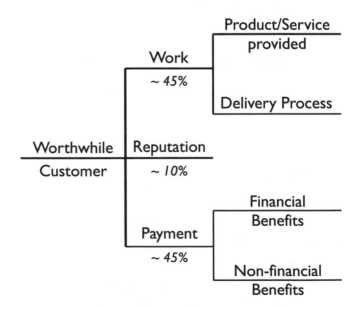

EXHIBIT 7.3. Value and its drivers, for Suppliers (operational Partnership). The concept of Value may be captured by the term Worthwhile Customer. The percentages indicate the relative importance likely to be ascribed to the three main drivers of Value, when data are collected.

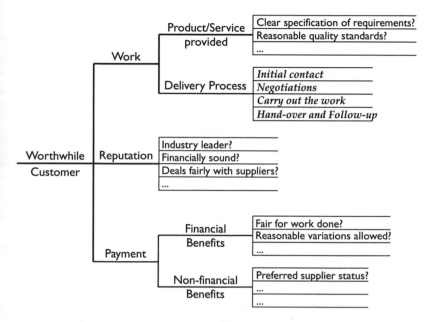

EXHIBIT 7.4. Elaboration of a prototypical Supplier Value tree.

data are collected. Exhibit 7.4 shows a typical elaboration of this Supplier Value tree, with details depending on the product or service provided.

What is Value for an Alliance?

For convenience, we'll use the term Alliance to refer to a Partnership of a tactical nature, recognizing that it may have a more specific interpretation in some situations.

There may be two or more Partners; and the Alliance may be of fixed duration: for example it may have been assembled to complete a major infrastructure project, or it may be an indefinite arrangement.

The principal drivers of *Alliance Value* differ from those for a Supplier Value tree, as can be seen in Exhibit 7.5, which also shows indicative Impact weights. In this model, *Sharing of Risk* appears as a driver of *Remuneration* arrangements, although for some alliances the Partners may think it is so important that it should be a direct driver of *Value*. An elaboration of this model is described shortly.

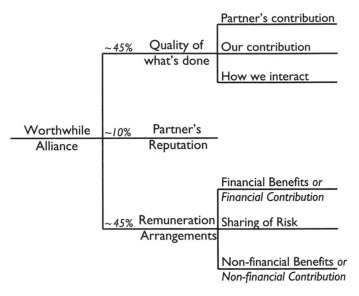

EXHIBIT 7.5. Value and its drivers for an Alliance (tactical Partnership). The concept of Value may be captured by the term Worthwhile Alliance. Sharing of Risk appears as a driver for Remuneration Arrangements in this example, although particular circumstances may warrant elevating it to the same level.

What is Value for a Co-venture?

We call a strategic Partnership a Co-venture. As suggested in Exhibit 7.1, the strategic aspect appears in terms of joint planning and commitments, full disclosure, sharing of results, information, resources, costs and rewards, and so on. There may be more than two partners to the Co-venture, but not nearly as many as is possible in many Alliances.

The *Co-venture Value* tree in Exhibit 7.6 shows that the principal drivers of Partnership Value are distinctively different. This is pointed up by the indicative Impact weights: *they place primary emphasis on the quality of the relationship.*

Again, the driver relating to *Sharing of Risk* can appear in various ways, depending on how the Partners view its importance. It might be a driver of *Benefits from the Relationship* or of *Quality of*

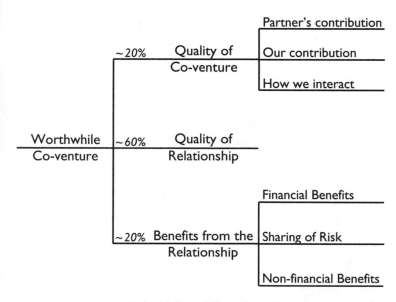

EXHIBIT 7.6. Value and its drivers, for a Co-venture (strategic Partnership). The concept of Value is captured by the term Worthwhile Co-venture. Sharing of Risk appears as a driver for Benefits, though the Partners could choose to position it elsewhere, either as a driver of Quality of Relationship or directly as a driver of Value.

Relationship, or even a direct driver of *Value*, at the same level as these other two.

7.5 MANAGING PARTNERSHIP VALUE IN PRACTICE

Managing Partnership Value presents an interesting situation when it comes to collecting data: in most cases, there aren't very many people to provide the data. The whole process is a lot more personal – just like it was for managing Key Accounts, and as it will be when we look at how to manage Owner Value.

Managing Supplier Value

Some companies have many small suppliers, all providing a very similar service. For example, your company's products may be distributed using a franchise model for which a common Supplier Value tree may be appropriate. In this case, just use the methods you use for

Customers and People: develop the details for the Value tree (Exhibit 7.3) using Focus Groups of suppliers, then collect the data, analyze, report and act – not forgetting to let your suppliers know what you're doing to improve things.

However, with just a few suppliers, you'll need to find out the detailed information from each of them, possibly individually if they are providing quite different products or services. The process is then similar to managing Alliance Value.

Managing Alliance or Co-venture Value

Again, the number of partners matters. With just two or three, it is feasible to develop complete trees. For example, Exhibit 7.7 is a

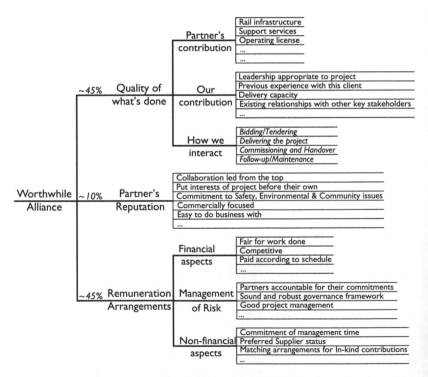

EXHIBIT 7.7. Prototypical elaboration of an Alliance Value tree (tactical Partnership). The details are obtained from interviews with the Alliance Partners.

prototypical elaboration of Exhibit 7.5, based on interviews with two partners in an Alliance to carry out the mining development project (B).

The Antarctic Climate and Ecosystems Cooperative Research Centre (ACE CRC) is a multidisciplinary partnership of twenty-one national and international organizations. Its mission is to provide science, knowledge and understanding to help Australia meet the challenges of climate change.[2]

The partners are drawn from academic, government and private sectors. Between them, they provide a unique and complementary combination of skills, knowledge, operational capabilities, commercial outlook and political perspective, ranging from world-class scientists to highly placed government officials, to a scientific research vessel and logistical support appropriate for operating in the Southern Ocean and Antarctica.

Because of the nature of the CRC program,[3] funding is only available for five to seven years at a time, so the ACE CRC has had three manifestations in its nineteen years of existence. However, no further extensions are possible, so if this very successful research collaboration is to continue in two years' time, some other form of Co-venture, preferably one of a more permanent nature, will need to be created.

Accordingly, the CEO of ACE, Dr Tony Press, commissioned a Partnership Value study "to provide information that contributes to enhancing the value of the ACE CRC partnership both for ACE and for each of the partners in our collaboration, especially as we look to 2014."

It was decided that the study should focus on five of the six core partners (the sixth being based in Germany), plus the core group of researchers in the CRC itself (as distinct from those in each partner organization), giving a total of six partners. It was not feasible to develop a Value tree for each of the fifteen interactions between partners, let alone have each partner fill in five surveys. So the following two views were selected for study:

1. Each partner's view of the Value provided by the CRC for that partner.
2. The view of the CRC leadership about the Value provided by each partner to the CRC.

In view of its current structure, a tactical partnership model was selected for each of these views.

For (1), the general structure of the Value tree is shown in Exhibit 7.8. Two senior officers from each partner organization were interviewed to provide the Attributes appropriate to that partner.

For (2), a simpler Value tree was used, without customization, as shown in Exhibit 7.9.

For the partner views, each of the officers involved in developing the Value tree was invited to complete a web-based survey based on their partner-specific Value trees. Responses were obtained from all partners. Two additional "business impact" questions were included, relating to:

- Willingness to collaborate with these partners in another joint venture
- Willingness to recommend these partners to others.

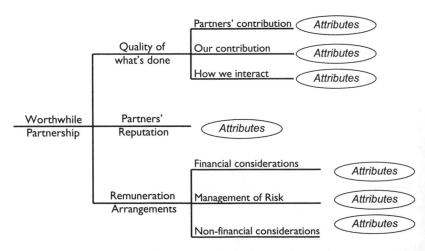

EXHIBIT 7.8. Structure of Value tree used to represent a partner's view of the Value provided by the ACE CRC. It represents a tactical form for the relationship.

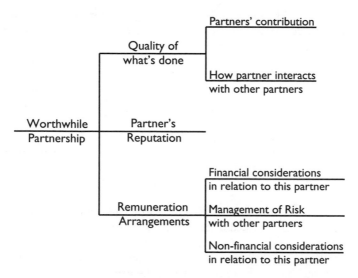

EXHIBIT 7.9. Structure of Value tree used to represent the CRC's view of the Value provided by a partner. This tree was not customized for each partner (no Attributes associated with the main branches).

For the CRC view, the CEO and Deputy CEO completed a survey about how they perceived each partner organization added Value to the CRC.

The overall top-level partner responses, averaged over all partners, are shown in Exhibit 7.10. All ratings are high. The two "business impact" questions were also rated highly, 9.3 and 9.0 respectively.

There is little guidance here about what might need improvement, so we look at whether the scores were consistently high across all partners. Exhibit 7.11 shows this table and the next-level tables for each of the six partners.

Apart from an isolated rating of 6, the ratings lie in a narrow range of 7 to 10 on the scale 1–10. Is everything really so rosy? The only way to check is to look below the surface.

Since 7 is effectively the lowest rating in Exhibit 7.11, we studied all the Attributes that had been assigned a rating in the range 1 to 7 in the lower-level tables. There turned out to be quite a few of these. Two questions arise immediately:

EXHIBIT 7.10. The top-level Partner Value profile for ACE CRC. Quality of Work is the dominant driver of overall satisfaction with the Partnership as being worthwhile. All ratings are high.

Driver	Impact weight	Rating
Quality of Work	49%	8.5
Partners' Reputation	29%	8.3
Remuneration Arrangements	22%	8.6
Worthwhile Partnership		8.8

EXHIBIT 7.11. Ratings for Worthwhile Partnership and its drivers, and the next-level tables, provided by each of the six Partners. Nearly all the ratings are in the range 8–10. NA (Not applicable) relates to a government department for which aspects of Remuneration did not apply. The corresponding Impact weights were broadly comparable across the Partners.

	Partner					
	1	2	3	4	5	6
Partners' Contribution	9	8	8	8	8	8.5
Own Contribution	9	8	8	6	8	8.5
Interaction	7	8	8	9	8	9
Quality of Work	9	9	8	8	8	9
Financial Considerations	9	8.5	9	9	8	9
Management of Risk	8	7.5	8	8	8	9
Non-financial Considerations	9	7.5	8	9	8	9
Remuneration Arrangements	9	9	NA	8	8	9
Quality	9	9	8	8	8	9
Reputation	8	7.5	9	8	8	9
Remuneration	9	9	NA	8	8	9
Value	9	8	9	9	8	10

1. If there are lower ratings at the lower level, why can't their effect be seen in the ratings at the higher level?
2. Were there any general themes associated with the lower ratings?

As to the first question, one plausible explanation is that, overall, the people involved in the CRC were desperately keen that a long, enjoyable and successful collaboration continue indefinitely, although it is by no means clear how a future Partnership might be constituted, let alone funded indefinitely.

Concerning the second question, an important strategic issue did manifest itself: with a few exceptions, the low ratings corresponded to Attributes of the relationship between the Partners. The reason why this was *strategic* was that the current CRC is looking to morph into a strategic Partnership within a couple of years. And in the strategic model for a Partnership (Exhibit 7.6), *Quality of relationship* is the dominant driver of overall Value.

How did the CEO respond to these results?[4]

It is not surprising that, overall, the core partners rated the collaboration highly. After all, the CRC has been in existence for two decades and the core partners have been engaged together in 4 iterations of the collaboration. During this period the ACE CRC has established very strong scientific and institutional links that are recognised nationally and internationally. The CRC funding has provided benefit to each of the core partners, allowing them to collaborate in the partnership, and, at the same time get value from it directly. The top level responses to the survey provide evidence of this: each partner rated the value of the partnership to them highly.

Looking in detail at the responses where ratings were 7 or less, reviewing these with the partners, and assessing the comments provided against these criteria during the survey, three themes emerged which are important to consider in any future collaboration.

The first is that the cost of transaction in the partnership is uneven. Some of the core partners are "more expensive" to engage with than others simply because they are required to meet Government set revenue targets and charge higher overheads on their participation. Some of the lower rating scores reflected this fact, but not to the extent that it was prejudicial to future collaboration – it was merely noted as a fact that influenced the relative score given.

The second theme to emerge from these lower scores was that of "sharing of profile". In a partnership that engages nationally recognised institutions such as CSIRO or the Australian Antarctic Division, and the host institution, the University of Tasmania, branding the joint efforts inside ACE (or any other CRC or similar partnership) is often a difficult job – when is the award-winning scientist identified in the media as ACE or CSIRO? When is the significant research voyage to the Antarctic characterised as an ACE voyage or an AAD activity? How does the nascent Institute for Marine and Antarctic Studies at the University of Tasmania differentiate itself from the ACE CRC? The ratings that reflect on these issues were, once again, not fatal to the building of future collaborations – well-established protocols and the existence of a high level of good will ensure that these matters are able to be managed successfully to everyone's ultimate benefit.

The third theme to emerge was the balance in the collegial relationships between partners. The ratings and comments associated with collegiality indicated that some partners felt that one or more of the other partners were less collegial than the rest. While, once again, the ratings did not indicate that these lower scores were fatal to future collaboration and partnership, and this was confirmed in follow-up discussions with respondents, most partners felt that collegiality was a very important component of value that the ACE provides. Lack of collegiality was seen to de-value present and future partnerships, and could be fatal to long term institutional collaboration.

The partnership value process reflects the value of a long and productive relationship, and clearly points to the importance of the quality of the relationships among partners in building a future collaboration.

We'll talk about how to run the all-important planning workshop in Chapter 13 (Section 13.6). This is where you develop a good understanding of what the data are telling you, identify your priorities, allocate resources, make sure someone is responsible for getting things moving, and plan how you'll communicate what you're doing to those who need to know.

7.6 CODA: BEING A DEMANDING CUSTOMER

Every enterprise has a lot of money going out the door to its suppliers, who may be operational, tactical or strategic, and you want a fair value exchange from each.

Companies like Toyota and Walmart don't wait for their suppliers to survey them. They make clear what their Value needs are. Is it time for you to screen your own suppliers for this purpose?

NOTES

1 As evidence of the fact that that there is a continuum of partnership models along the Interaction axis, Normann (2001, page 38) has described an interesting partnership model for a distributor of pharmaceutical products to independent pharmacies. Whilst losing a single pharmacy is not at all critical to the distributor's success, there is a strong focus on what Normann calls co-production of value by the supplier (distributor) and the supplier's customers (pharmacies) for the end-user.

Dull *et al.* (1995) described an even wider spectrum of partnerships, from a "Straight sale" to "Unification." The former is characterized by little or no transfer of information, and few or no deep relationships. There is effectively no relationship to manage. The latter is effectively the same as the Strategic relationship described here.

2 From the ACE CRC web site (www.acecrc.org.au/):

"ACE is built on a strong, long-standing and productive collaboration between six core partners. It also has 15 supporting partners. Four of the supporting partners in ACE are commercial. These commercial collaborations underline the increasing recognition of the potential commercial impacts of climate change.

"ACE has a long history as a CRC. ACE was originally established as the 'CRC for the Antarctic and Southern Ocean Environment' in 1991 in the first round of funding for Australia's Cooperative Research Centres Program. Since then, it has been refunded in 1997 (as the CRC for Antarctica and the Southern Ocean), and in 2003 and 2010 as the ACE CRC."

3 From the CRC Association web site (crca.asn.au/): "The CRC Program was established in 1990 to improve the effectiveness of Australia's research effort through bringing together researchers in the public and private sectors with the end users. The CRC Program links researchers with industry and government with a focus towards research application. The close interaction between researchers and the end users is the defining characteristic of the Program. Moreover, it allows end users to help plan the direction of the research as well as to monitor its progress."

4 I am most grateful to Dr Tony Press, CEO of the ACE CRC, for providing this assessment.

8   Adding Value for the Community

It's a commonly held adage that successful businesses are good for the community. What is not always so well understood is that successful communities are good for business.

Richard Pratt[1]

PART I   COMMUNITY VALUE AND BUSINESS IMPACT

8.1   PREAMBLE

Is your enterprise regarded as a good corporate citizen?

Does it give your industry a good name or a bad name?

How do you know that the "good deeds" you perform as part of discharging your "Corporate Social Responsibility" are having any impact on the success or otherwise of your business?

In fact, are you doing anything in this area that reflects your company's concerns about its impact on the local community, or about preserving the environment, or efforts in pursuit of the betterment of humanity locally or globally?

Amazingly, with all the stunning examples of very successful people and corporations who have been putting something back into the community, there are still many enterprises that "don't get it."

On the one hand, the Bill and Melinda Gates Foundation provides very considerable financial support for projects directed at improving global health, reducing poverty and aiding development. Warren Buffett, investor *extraordinaire*, has announced that his accumulated wealth will be donated to the Foundation.

On the other hand, Michael Lynch, former Chief Executive of London's Southbank Centre, who oversaw the £118 million redevelopment of the Royal Festival Hall, commented that.

> [his] greatest disappointment had been corporate Britain's failure to back worthy causes at a time of unprecedented excess, and that those who had benefited from huge salaries and bonuses must return more to society
>
> ...
>
> When Macquarie Bank lost their bid for the London Stock Exchange I asked a number of their Australian Directors why they hadn't seen fit to support philanthropic activity in London but they seemed not to see how it may have helped them in their quest.[2]

The opportunities – and requirements – for being a good corporate citizen are remarkably diverse.

Carrying out a massive infrastructure project, whether it be a major freeway, a gas pipeline or a mine site, must involve having an ongoing dialog with the communities it is disrupting. Winning future contracts may depend critically on how well the impact on the environment and the legacy of the project (smokestack emissions, leakages, run-offs *etc.*) have been managed.

A chemical factory operating near a community will survive only if it maintains its impact on its surroundings at an acceptable level, on an ongoing basis.

Proposals to release GM crops require permissions from a range of stakeholders: other farmers, local communities, prospective consumers, and even other countries to which crops and their derivatives are exported.

These are the more obvious situations, in which tangible products are produced. The situation with services is rather less obvious but no less important in terms of business outcomes.

In the measurement context, the starting point is the same as for other stakeholders: *what does it mean to add Value for the Community?*

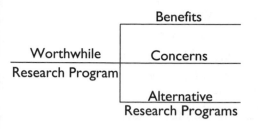

EXHIBIT 8.1. An example of Community Value and its drivers, for a research agency carrying out research into methods for managing pest animals. The concept of Value is captured by the term Worthwhile Research Program.

8.2 WHAT IS VALUE FOR THE COMMUNITY?

Depending on the nature of your enterprise, Community Value can be modeled in a wide variety of ways. One fairly general approach is to express Value in terms of the perceived Benefits and Concerns of your presence or activities.

Exhibit 8.1 shows the top section of a Community Value tree for a research agency carrying out research into GM viruses to manage pest mice. We'll discuss it shortly. The concept of Value is captured by the term *Worthwhile Research Program*, with two drivers – Benefits and Concerns – that tend to be present in all models, and a third that is specific to the situation.

In other situations, Image may be a suitable third driver. For example, if you are running a Guggenheim Museum, it is likely that Image would be important to the local community. For rather different reasons, Image may also be an issue if you operate a major chemical plant near a residential area.

8.3 LINKING COMMUNITY VALUE TO BUSINESS PERFORMANCE

As always, you need to know how this is going to help your business. And as before, it can be done by connecting overall Community Value to higher-level business drivers using Value–Loyalty graphs, where Loyalty will depend on the nature of your enterprise, or on the proposition presented to the Community. For example:

a. If you are running a Guggenheim Museum, you may want to link Value to *Willingness to support extended hours of operation*.

b. For a chemical plant, linking Value to *Willingness to support construction of an extension to the plant* may be appropriate.

c. If your company is developing a GM grain, linking Value to *Willingness to support commercial production of the grain in this region* is likely to be of interest.

d. If you're operating in a regulated industry, such as power, Community support is important for rate reviews and increases, construction of power lines, and so on, so *Willingness to speak favorably* is an important issue.

Obtaining competitive data, or even comparable data from elsewhere, may not be possible, so this may be the only way that you can benchmark effectively. In case (c), you might need government approval to release the grain commercially, and government approval may be contingent upon, say, 80 percent of the community supporting release. If, during the process of managing Community Value, you can't raise the Value score to a level commensurate with this level of community support, the message is: *don't waste your money scaling up to production.* You'll never be able to sell the wheat commercially in this region.

PART II MANAGING COMMUNITY VALUE

8.4 MANAGING COMMUNITY VALUE IN PRACTICE

Plagues of mice are disasters much feared by Australian wheat farmers. They occur every few years, after plentiful rain. Warm conditions and a good grain crop provide ideal breeding conditions. The mouse population can explode, leading to what can only be described as rivers of mice flowing through farmhouses devouring everything their teeth can cope with. These mice are an introduced species; native mice do not eat grain.

One method proposed for managing these explosions was to develop a version of a 'common cold' mouse virus genetically modified so as to make female mice sterile. The idea was that when a population started increasing in numbers, the virus would be introduced to prevent it growing out of control. Of course, development and testing of such a virus raises several community issues, so a Community Value survey was developed[3] to ascertain the community's perceptions, as a prelude to developing a public awareness program.

The Community Value tree developed as the basis of the survey is shown in Exhibit 8.2, without the third driver.

Some 'business impact' questions were included at the end of the survey, relating to:

- Willingness to support the use of this method for control of mice (*i.e.* commercial release)
- Willingness to support research into viral methods for control of other pests such as rabbits and foxes
- Importance of the community being consulted on research like this.

Top-level results for the survey are shown in Exhibit 8.3. The overall Value score of 8.2 is largely influenced by the perceived benefits of reducing the impact of the mice.

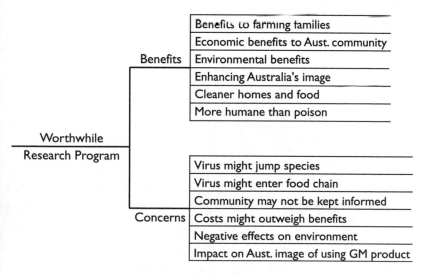

EXHIBIT 8.2. Community Value tree used as the basis for a study of community perceptions about research into a genetically modified virus for managing pest mice. Each Attribute had some elaboration to explain its meaning.

EXHIBIT 8.3. Top-level results from the Community Value survey relating to GM viral control of pest mice. The overall Value score is 8.2, with the main driver being the perceived Benefits of the research program. The ratings are on a 10-point scale, where 1 = Poor and 10 = Excellent, for Benefits, and 1 = Very concerned and 10 = Unconcerned, for Concerns about the research.

Driver	Impact weight (%)	Mean rating (precision ± 0.20)
Benefits	84	8.3
Concerns	16	6.6
Value		8.2

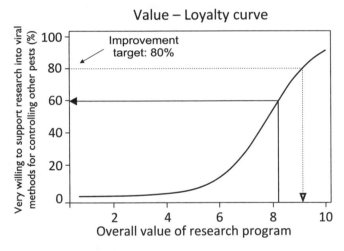

EXHIBIT 8.4. Linking the overall mean rating on Community Value to a higher-level business driver. An overall Value score of 8.2 corresponds to some 60 percent of the community very willing to support similar research to manage other pest animals. If community support needs to be at least 80 percent, this implies that the overall Value score will need to be lifted to around 9.1, providing a meaningful target for a community dialog process.

How good is a Value score of 8.2?

Exhibit 8.4 shows that it corresponds to about 60 percent of the Community being very willing to support exploring similar approaches to managing other pest animals.

Further, if you think that you need at least 80 percent community support to justify a further bid for funding, this would mean that the Value score would have to reach about 9.1. So you set about trying to achieve this by using the lower-level data to identify where to focus communication activities and, possibly, to identify further research to be done.

8.5 CONTINUOUS MONITORING COMMUNITY VALUE SURVEYS

Continuous monitoring surveys are ideal for managing Community Value. Because they are intended to inform public awareness and dialog activities, they can provide timely feedback about how well your communication initiatives are working, as well as identifying emerging issues and allowing you to make a timely intervention.

As an example, the Invasive Animals Cooperative Research Centre in Australia launched a national weekly survey of the community's attitudes towards invasive animals and the methods being proposed to manage them. Some forty respondents of different ages, education level and genders were recruited each week to participate.[4]

One survey question asked respondents to rate the top five pest animals (from a list of twenty-six pests presented to them). Rabbits featured among the top few, and feral camels were eleventh on the list.[5]

In each case, an intervention was made: publication of a major report, in the case of camels, and a six-month "rabbit awareness" campaign, in the case of rabbits. As can be seen from Exhibit 8.5, the effects of the two campaigns were reflected almost immediately in the survey results (C and R denoting, respectively, the intervention points for the camel and rabbit campaigns). It is remarkable that with such sparse data, effective monitoring is possible.

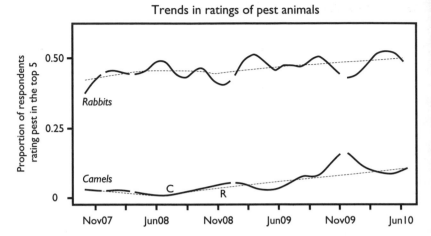

EXHIBIT 8.5. Time series showing how the percentage of people rating two invasive species, rabbits (higher series) and camels as being among the top five pests, changed over time. Each series shows an increase after pest-specific communication activities were introduced, with the symbols R(abbits) and C(amels) indicating approximate timing of the interventions. Gaps appear in the series because no data were collected around the end of the year. Dotted lines have been added to emphasise the changes in trends.

NOTES

1 Richard Pratt – former Chairman of Visy Industries, and founder of the Pratt Foundation, a world-wide charitable organization. The quote appeared in an article entitled "Doing the right things is good for business," *The Sun-Herald*, January 25, 2004.

2 "Arts, Life and Credit Crunches: Reflections on the last seven years away from Australia." Speech by Michael Lynch, CBE, AM, to the Currency House/ Australia Business Arts Foundation Arts and Public Life Breakfast, July 7, 2009 at the Sofitel Melbourne on Collins; see: www.currencyhouse.org.au/sites/ default/files/transcripts/Arts,%20Life%20&%20Credit%20Crunches.pdf.

3 See Fisher, Cribb and Peacock (2008) for a full description of the project.

4 See Fisher, Lee and Cribb (2012).

5 Rabbits have been destroying the Australian environment and farming and grazing land for many decades. The environmental devastation caused by camels in arid areas is a more recent phenomenon. There are currently about one million feral camels in central Australia.

9 Adding Value for the Owners

However beautiful the strategy, you should occasionally look at the results.

W. S. Churchill

Wilful blindness: "If there is knowledge that you could have had and should have had but chose not to have, you are still responsible."

Margaret Heffernan[1]

9.1 PREAMBLE: WHO'S THE OWNER?

Who owns your business?

What Value are you creating for the Owners that prevents them from investing their money elsewhere? In fact, what does Value mean to them?

Answers to the first question tend to fall into one of four categories:

1. Shareholders of publicly listed companies
2. Individuals or families or groups, for privately owned enterprises
3. Governments, for a wide range of official departments, statutory authorities and other agencies
4. Communities, for a range of community-based cooperatives.

The diversity of types of ownership implies a diversity of concepts of Value for the Business. Here, we'll concentrate on publicly listed companies, as they present the greatest complexity.

The complexity arises partly because, by and large, the shareholders are *not* entitled to receive all the information they need to assess the Value being created for them. That's not a surprise: companies need to keep a lot of information confidential to develop and maintain competitive advantage. So, as proxy for the shareholders, public companies have Boards, members of which *are* entitled to have access to all the information. That's why we develop the Value tree for the Board, rather than for the shareholders.

Two things emerge from working out the meaning of Value for the Owners of the enterprise:

- The first is, of course, the Board Value tree. This can be used by the Board as the basis for a yearly evaluation of the performance of the leadership.
- The second is the Holy Grail of performance measurement. We have identified the first essential deliverable of a measurement system specified in Exhibit 2.1: *a concise overview of the health of your organization.*

And there are two other issues that receive much less attention that we'll discuss later in this chapter:

- Timing – the simultaneous reporting of both financial *and* non-financial information.
- The relationship between the Board and the executive leadership. What is the Board doing to help the company carry out its business? Or, if you like: *how does the Board itself add Value for the executive leadership?*

9.2 WHAT IS VALUE FOR THE BOARD OF A LISTED COMPANY?

There are a number of purely financial metrics purporting to be measures of Shareholder Value. The point about each of them is that, by and large, they are "hard" numbers calculated from accounting statements and stock price data. For example, EVA (Economic Value Added) is claimed by some to be the ultimate quantity on which to base investment decisions.

The whole thesis of this book is that the ultimate performance measures are *perceptual*, measures of *perceived Value* that implicitly or explicitly form the basis of our decision-making. Hard numbers blend with gut feelings, rumors, fears, superstitions, and a host of other environmental factors, out of which crystallizes a choice.

The Business Value tree that we'll develop, and the derived KPIs, contains just the information that shareholders really need; however, shareholders can only ever guess at what this might be, whereas Board members have direct access to it.

And so to defining *Value* for the Board: *All things considered, is this enterprise a Worthwhile Investment for Shareholders?* We postulate that there are three principal drivers of Value – shareholders' perceptions of:

- the *Return on Resources Invested*,
- the *Wellness* of the company's assets, and
- the *Risk* associated with investment in the company

as shown in the top section of the Shareholder Value tree in Exhibit 9.1. There is no need to look for connections between Business Value and higher-level business drivers: this is the top level! So, the next question is: how do we elaborate each of these drivers, to create a full Business Value tree?

9.3 BUILDING THE VALUE TREE

Exhibit 9.2 illustrates a fairly generic Business Value tree. Depending on the nature of your business – manufacturing products, construction, extraction, services *etc.* – the details may vary but the basic structure remains fixed.

Worthwhile Investment	Return on Resources Invested
	Wellness
	Risk

EXHIBIT 9.1. Top level of the Business Value tree for the Board of a public enterprise. The concept of Value is captured by the term Worthwhile Investment.

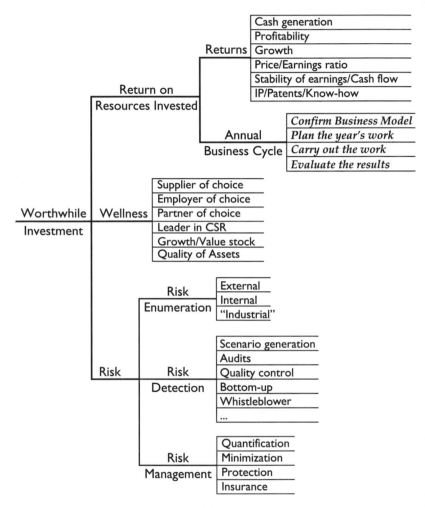

EXHIBIT 9.2. Value and its drivers for the Board. Return is elaborated in terms of financial and non-financial performance quantities and assets, and the key business process which, for the Board, is the annual planning cycle. Risk is so important that it is elevated to the same status as Return and Wellness.

As a generic structure, this tree needs to be adapted to fit your enterprise. Let's look at a few branches of the tree.

- The Attributes of *Returns* will vary, depending on the nature of your business; for example, *IP/Patents/Know-how* may not be important considerations in some industries, whereas they may be the critical Attributes in others. See Section 9.6 for further comment. Leadership preferences also play a part here: some leaders may regard EVA as a key Attribute of *Returns*; others prefer different metrics.

- *Risk Enumeration* is shown here with three basic categories:
  ○ *External Risks*, *e.g.* environmental, political, agency (i.e. exposure through partnerships),
  ○ *Internal Risks*, *e.g.* fraud, intellectual property, "Industrial" *Risks*, *e.g.* technology change, competitive strength, loss of key supplier, safety, statutory reporting.

Again, this part of the tree can be re-shaped to have more branches, depending on what's important to your company.

- There are several approaches to *Risk Detection*, only some of which are shown here.

Of course, the Attributes may also change depending on the state of evolution of the enterprise. Consider a minerals exploration and mining company that was seeking to exploit a metal deposit they discovered in South-east Asia. The Business Value study was conducted at a critical juncture, with funding tight and contingent on gaining operating permits from the appropriate authorities.

The Value tree, developed with the Chairman and Chief Financial Officer, is shown in Exhibit 9.3. However, the customization doesn't end here. Lower-level detail has been developed to clarify the precise meanings of a number of the Attributes, as shown in Exhibit 9.4.

Now we need some data.

9.4 USING THE BUSINESS VALUE TREE FOR BOARD ASSESSMENT OF ENTERPRISE PERFORMANCE

How can this Value tree provide Value to the Board itself?

It can do this by displaying in the simplest terms every Board member's individual perception of the state of the enterprise, and so reveal where the Board has a common view, and where there is

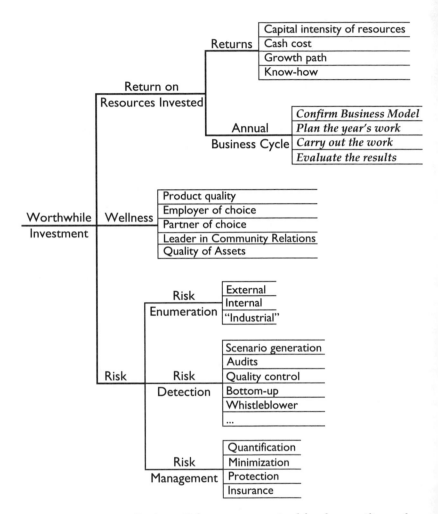

EXHIBIT 9.3. Business Value tree customized for the specific needs of a minerals exploration and mining company at a particular stage of development. See Exhibit 9.4 for elaboration of specific Attributes.

significant divergence of opinion that will have to be resolved to create alignment.

How are the data to be collected? It's obviously not sensible to survey the shareholders, as they haven't got access to the company's confidential information and so can't make an informed assessment.

Returns	Capital intensity of resources	e.g. development costs
	Cash cost	e.g. projected operating costs
	Growth path	e.g. perceived growth potential
	Know-how	e.g. skills, Intellectual Property

Wellness	Product quality	e.g. consistent high product quality (quantified)
	Employer of choice	e.g. attract and keep top people (quantified)
	Partner of choice	e.g. Partnership Value score
	Leader in Community Relations	e.g. Community Value score
	Quality of Assets	e.g. rank against peers

External Risk
- Environmental
- Political – security of titles
- Takeover
- Regulatory – timely grant of permits
- Catastrophic weather
- Metal price
- Oil price

Internal Risk
- Financing
- Governance
- Fraud

"Industrial" Risk
- Process Failure Heaps: Percolation, leaching
- Loss of key people
- Asian Partner Relations
- Safety

EXHIBIT 9.4. Elaboration of some Attributes in the Business Value tree in Exhibit 9.3. When the tree is used as the basis of a Business Value survey, the additional details clarify the meaning of the Attribute.

Instead, you have to ask their proxies, the members of the Board. In other words, the Business Value tree forms the basis of an assessment instrument that the Board uses to evaluate the executive leadership of the enterprise. It means that the Board members need, collectively, to have broad experience on Boards of other companies with some similarities to your company.

Also, the assessment needs to be synchronized with the planning and commitment process.

An assessment *led by an external facilitator* can be made once a year, or once every second year, depending on business requirements, using the following process:

1. The facilitator holds an initial discussion with the Board, introducing the overall concept, and developing the precise form of the Value tree appropriate to the enterprise.
2. The facilitator develops a simple survey instrument to capture quantitative and qualitative data (exactly as with Customer Value surveys).
3. Individual Board members complete the survey, rating the performance of the company and also their perceptions of performance for other companies for the main branches of the tree. They are also asked to allocate Impact weights for the higher-level branches; for example, to split 100 points between *Returns* and *Annual Business Cycle*, to indicate their relative importance in terms of driving *Returns on Resources Invested*. The facilitator summarizes the data, highlighting significant variations in responses.
4. The summary (excluding Board members' comments) is distributed in advance, suitably anonymized.
5. The facilitator conducts a Board planning workshop to help Board members to develop understanding of the results, resolve significant differences in ratings, and make preliminary identification of improvement priorities.

Exhibit 9.5 shows a prototypical top-level Business Value competitive profile resulting from summarizing the responses.

Actual results for a Business Value survey using the trees shown in Exhibit 9.3 and 9.4 are shown in Exhibit 9.6, based on data provided by the seven Board members. Insufficient competitive data were available to provide meaningful comparison so this part has been omitted.

Why were there such wildly differing results for the overall Value score, with one Board member rating Value as 9 and another as 4? Some key reasons appeared in the associated comments:

- (rating of Value = 9) "Permitting will be delivered and there will then be a significant value increase in the company."

EXHIBIT 9.5. A top-level Business Value competitive profile. The ratings are on a 10-point scale, where 1 = Poor and 10 = Excellent. The Impact weights were allocated beforehand. Based on scores from nine Board members, the overall Value score for your enterprise is 7.4, compared with your competition, which averages 7.7, so the Business Value Added (BVA) score is below par at 96%.

| Driver | Impact weight (%) | Mean rating and ranges | | Relative rating (%) |
		Your company	Competition	
Return on Resources Invested	41 (20–60)	7.8 (6–9)	8.3 (7–9)	104 (78–140)
Wellness	28 (10–33)	8.2 (6–9)	8.2 (7–9)	101 (80–150)
Risk	30 (20–50)	7.7 (5–9)	8.2 (7–9)	92 (60–114)
Value to the Shareholder		7.7	8.3	107

EXHIBIT 9.6. The top-level Business Value profile for the mineral exploration company. There are very clear discrepancies in the responses, indicating substantially differing views amongst the Board members.

Drivers of Business Value	Impact weight	Mean rating
Return on Resources Invested	42% (15–60)	5.4 (3–7)
Wellness	27% (15–40)	7.3 (6–9)
Risk	31% (20–70)	6.4 (4–8)
Value to the Shareholder		7.1 (4–9)

EXHIBIT 9.7. Classification of issues resulting from discussion of Business Value tree data.

		Importance		
		Low	Medium	High
Urgency	Low		6	
	Medium		1, 3, 7	8,2
	High		4, 5	2, 9

- (rating of Value score = 4) "The objective is driving returns for shareholders from all rounds of financing. Project and permitting delays and cost over-runs have led to shareholder dilution over the last few years. The company has cash through the end of November and is likely to need to have to further dilute shareholders prior to raising project finance. With a focus on permitting and feasibility, a lack of focus has been paid to the more mundane aspects of the company."

A discussion about these differences and about the variations in the Impact weights led to an agreed set of Impact weights: 40 percent; 20 percent; 40 percent. It also elicited a number of issues for further consideration.

Similar analysis of lower-level tables and associated comments produced several more issues, initially classified using the simple matrix format shown in Exhibit 9.7. The resulting list was then consolidated to produce a set of key action points (Exhibit 9.8), and the Board assigned rankings on the scale 1–3 to these points based on the criteria *Importance* and *Urgency*, with a ranking of 1 = relatively Low, and 3 = High, where:

- *High urgency* = action in next few weeks/months
- *Medium urgency* = action within 6 months
- *Low urgency* = can wait up to a year.

One final point: isn't Issue 6 in Exhibit 9.8 rather trivial for this level of discussion? In fact, *No it isn't*. Such behavior can mean:

Exhibit 9.8. Output from Board analysis of Value survey results. Importance and Urgency were each ranked on a 3-point scale with 1 = Low, 3 = High. "Strategic" and "Tactical" indicate who is responsible for action – the Board or the Executive. (Resourcing was not discussed at this Board meeting so the column is blank.)

Issue/Action	Importance	Urgency	Strategic/ Tactical	(Resources required)
1. Past performance versus future growth path? Why are we where we are?	2	2	S	
2. Financing strategy.	3	3	S / T	
3. How to manage expectations in the future?	2	2	T	
4. SE Asian – Australian interface.	2	3	S	
5. PR issue about ability to carry out the project.	2	3	T	
6. Discussion at Board closed down too quickly.	2	1	S / T	
7. Risk assessment.	2	2	T	
8. Are systems and processes in place to enable company to move forward when permitting achieved?	3	2	T	
9. Board review to position itself for next phase.	3	3	S	
10. Senior Management structure.	3	2	S / T	

- opportunities are being lost
- bad decision-making
- damage to relationships between Board members, and between the Board and the Executive.

9.5 HOW DOES THE BOARD ADD VALUE FOR THE LEADERSHIP OF THE ENTERPRISE?

As Chairman of the Board, do you know what your executive leadership expect from you by way of assistance? Or how well you are providing it?

As CEO, does your Board know what support you'd like? How well are you communicating your needs?

You can get answers to both these questions using a simple Value process that we'll just sketch. It follows very familiar lines.

Exhibit 9.9 shows a representation of Leadership Value in terms of three drivers:

- *Quality*: What does a Board have to do well, to enable you and your colleagues to do your best work?

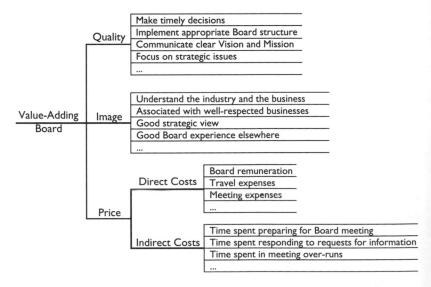

EXHIBIT 9.9. Leadership Value tree, showing the sorts of drivers and Attributes that may be important in determining how well the Board supports the enterprise in pursuing its mission.

- *External Image*: What's important about the make-up of the Board when viewed by people outside the enterprise, for example, by prospective investors, business partners, employees *etc.*?
- *Price*: Board members generally don't come free of charge. What does it really cost to have this Board?

As usual, it's probably best to have an external facilitator, who may be someone with senior leadership experience, to manage the process to:

1. develop the survey by first asking the Board what they think will be important to the leadership, then finding out from the leadership what the real Attributes are;
2. follow the Board process or the Key Account process described earlier, to prepare the survey, collect Impact weights, ratings and comments, and prepare a report;
3. conduct a planning workshop with the Board and the leadership, with the Board being asked to come up with their estimate of the results in the first instance, and then comparing these with the actual results. Identify priorities, actions and associated responsibilities, and plan how to communicate the outcomes;
4. conduct monitoring surveys annually.

9.6 VALUING INTANGIBLE ASSETS

In Exhibit 9.2, the indicative list of Attributes of *Returns* included some so-called "intangible assets" – IP/Patents/Know-how. Baruch Lev[2] defined an intangible asset as: "a claim to future benefits that does not have a physical or financial (a stock or a bond) embodiment," and added, in elaboration[3]

> intangible assets are nonphysical sources of value (claims to future benefits) generated by innovation (discovery), unique organizational designs, or human resources practices. Intangibles often interact with tangible and financial assets to create corporate value and economic growth.

... Intangible assets ... surpass physical assets in most enterprises, both in value and contribution to growth, yet they are routinely expenses in the financial reports and hence absent from corporate balance sheets. This asymmetric treatment of capitalizing (considered as assets) physical and financial investments while expensing intangibles leads to biased and deficient reporting of firms' performance and value.

Identifying good lead and lag indicators of intangible assets is very much a work in progress. The only intangibles that appear to feature regularly in quantified form in financial statements relate to "goodwill" and to "mast head" or brand name. Lev[4] provided some suggestions about possible indicators for a biotechnology company.

Of course, intangible assets take a variety of forms. Lev and co-workers[5] gave the following description of Lev's (2001) framework for intangible assets:

1. Discovery/learning intangibles – technology, know-how, patents and other assets emanating from the discovery (R&D) and learning (e.g. reverse engineering) processes of business enterprises, universities and national laboratories.
2. Customer-related intangibles – brands, trademarks and unique distribution channels (e.g. Internet-based sales), which create abnormal (above cost of capital) earnings.
3. Human-resource intangibles – specific human resource practices such as training and compensation systems, which enhance employee productivity and reduce turnover.
4. Organization capital – unique structural and organizational designs and business processes generating sustainable competitive advantages.

The last of these, organizational capital, is defined as[6]

the knowledge used to combine human skills and physical capital into systems for producing and delivering want-satisfying products.

The authors call organizational capital a "stealth asset" that explains the sustained superior performance of some companies compared with others:

> It is widely observed that within industries some companies systematically outperform their competitors and maintain their leading position for long periods of time, despite significant economic changes: Wal-Mart in retail, Microsoft in software, Southwest among airlines, DuPont in chemicals, Exxon in oil and gas, Intel in microprocessors, and the list goes on. Such superior performance in terms of growth in sales, earnings and stock returns cannot be attributed to monopoly power or government subsidies because these firms operate in a competitive environment. How can such enterprises achieve/maintain their superior performance and leading role? We argue that such enterprises have a stealth asset: organization capital – the agglomeration of business processes and systems, as well as a unique corporate culture, that enables them to convert factors of production into output more efficiently than competitors.

The authors developed a complex statistical measure of organizational capital and produced some examples showing that "the organizational capital measure is *associated* with five years of future operating and stock return performance, after controlling for other factors." (Emphasis added.) However, this is association, not causation (which the authors do *not* claim). There remains much work to be done.

9.7 CODA: INTEGRATED REPORTING

The entire focus of this book is on *internal* reporting, particularly regular reporting at Board and leadership levels.

Another form of reporting carried out by an enterprise is *external reporting*, for example, reports to shareholders, or mandatory reporting to regulators by government agencies on environmental matters and efficient use of energy.

More generally, there is increased emphasis on so-called "Integrated reporting," whereby an enterprise communicates regularly to the outside world about broad issues to do with its strategy, governance, performance and prospects. These reports are intended to include predictors not just of future financial performance and prospects but of other aspects of the enterprise; in particular, Environmental, Social and Corporate Governance (or ESG) reporting relates to sustainability and ethical impact. Robert Eccles[7] has provided a recent commentary on the future of sustainability reporting. Such information is, potentially, of great interest to investors in informing their investment strategy.

Of course, there can be a great difference between what an enterprise is prepared to make public in terms of its performance metrics, and the commercially sensitive metrics appearing in a monthly or quarterly report to a Board. That said, what appears in a publicly available integrated report will almost certainly draw upon metrics appearing in various places in the Board reports. For example, internal metrics related to environmental issues may appear under Community Value and also under Risk.

NOTES

1 "The Wilful Blindness of Rupert Murdoch"; available at: www.huffingtonpost.com/margaret-heffernan-/wilful-blindness-rupert-murdoch_b_898157.html.
2 Lev (2001), page 5.
3 *Ibid.*, page 7. Partly drawn from testimony to a hearing of the Senate Committee on Banking, Housing and Urban Affairs on July 19, 2000, relating to "Adapting a 1930s Financial Reporting model to the Twenty-First Century."
4 *Ibid.*, page 117.
5 Lev, Radhakrishnan and Zhang (2009).
6 Following Evenson and Westphal (1995).
7 Eccles (2012).

10 What to report and how to report it

The best of seers is he who guesses well.

Euripides[1]

Far better an approximate answer to the right question, which is often vague, than the exact answer to the wrong question, which can always be made precise.

John W. Tukey

10.1 PREAMBLE: WHERE ARE WE GOING?

Recall (from Chapter 1) that our purpose is to describe a system for performance measurement that gives you the quantitative information that you need to help you run your enterprise. "Quantitative information that you need" means information that is:

- timely[2]
- actionable – in a format (graphical or tabular) that facilitates decision-making
- measures the right thing, the right way
- clearly interpretable in terms of its limitations – degree of uncertainty in the measurement, possible biases.

And additionally, the information has to provide a concise overview of the health of your enterprise. So, what should be reported, and how should the reporting take place to make the most of this information?

10.2 CONCISE AND COMPREHENSIVE REPORTS

We are now in a position to identify the groups of measures that need to appear in monthly or quarterly leadership reports. The Board Value tree in Exhibit 9.2 identifies six groups of Attributes that need to be monitored, as shown in Exhibit 10.1, where "to be monitored" means that *lead indicators are needed.*

Reports that answer the question: "Where are we now?"

You're chairing the Board of a large retail company, in fact, a large group of companies. It operates in a number of countries and has

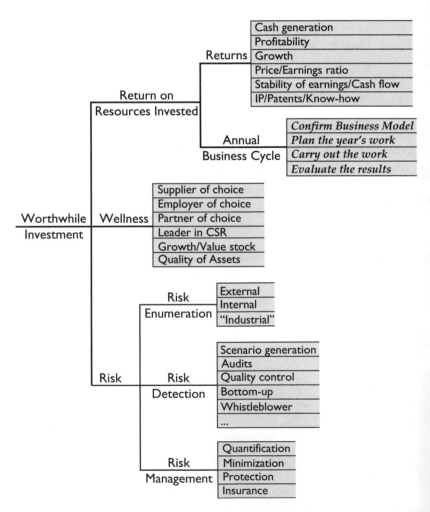

EXHIBIT 10.1. The Board Value tree helps to identify the specific groups of lead indicators (shaded in the exhibit) that need to be monitored regularly (*e.g.* monthly or quarterly) by the leadership, to provide a concise overview of where your enterprise is headed.

many business units and product lines. Where should the reporting start? Well, what's the overall picture?

Exhibits 10.2 and10.3 show the big picture.[3] They are presented as having hyper-linked capability to exploit current computer technology. Hard-copy versions would provide the graphs separately. There are two sets of reports: Owner Value metrics, and (other) Stakeholder Value metrics.

Owner Value metrics (Exhibit 10.2). These relate to Management of Resources and of Risk, two critical components of Owner (in this case, Shareholder) Value. The financial indicators are indicative of the sorts of standard indicators used[4] in the retail sector. Note that:

- many financial indicators are ratios, to facilitate benchmarking
- all indicators have precisions[5] and trend charts
- arrows indicate whether there has been any significant change since the last report.

The metric for overall Risk is based on metrics for its key components. The suggestion is that the metric for each component be reported as the *maximum* of all the corresponding values in the Business Units. Risk metrics are reported on the scale 0 (minimum) to 100 (maximum). If a specific risk is identified as sufficiently grave that it affects the viability of a Business Unit (*e.g.* potential loss of a permit to operate a lease, for a mining company), it is reported with a mark (!), and this mark must persist through all higher levels of aggregation to the top-level report, as shown in Exhibit 10.2. Because "!" appears with Risk Management, it must also appear with the overall Risk Level Assessment (RLA) metric.[6,7]

The indicators in Exhibit 10.2 reveal a satisfactory situation. For example:

- The significant movement in EBIT over the last quarter has brought it up to the target level. The other financial indicators are at or about the targets set for the end of June.
- There has been steady and sustained improvement in overall management of Risk (last panel in Exhibit 10.2). However, there is an alert (!) of a critical issue and it derives from how a particular risk

Stakeholder Value report: July 2015

Owner Value

Report level
| Group |
| Business Unit ... |
| Region ... |

Profitability	This quarter	Last quarter	Change		
EBIT	8.1% ⊕	7.9%	↑	⌁	
Return on Equity	12.2% ⊕	12.3%	→	⌁	
Gross Profit Margin	39.1% ⊕	41.2%	↓	⌁	
Sales per store	$0.90M ⊕	$0.85M	↑	⌁	
...	...	...	...	⌁	

EBIT (%)

Target
Jul 15

Show last
8 quarters

July '13   July '14   July '15

Solvency					
Current ratio	1.08 ⊕	1.04	→	⌁	
Net debt / Equity	18.0% ⊕	17.7%	→	⌁	
...	...	...	...	⌁	
...	...	...	...	⌁	
...	...	...	...	⌁	

Net debt / equity (%)

Target

Show last
8 quarters

July '13   July '14   July '15

Financial flexibility					
Lines of credit	$31M ⊕	$24M	↑	⌁	
Interest cover (×)	8.1 ⊕	7.6	→	⌁	
Debt maturities /mo.	$18 ⊕	$17	→	⌁	
[+ Solvency ratios listed above]	...	...	...	⌁	
...	...	...	...	⌁	

Interest cover (×)

Target

Show last
8 quarters

July '13   July '14   July '15

Asset-holding risk					
Stock markdowns	30.5% ⊕	27.1%	→	⌁	
...	...	...	→	⌁	
...	...	...	...	⌁	
...	...	...	...	⌁	
...	...	...	...	⌁	

Markdowns (%)

Show last
8 quarters

Target

July '13   July '14   July '15

Risk level assessment					
Overall risk 0 = min, 100 = max	26 !⊕	15	↑	⌁	
Enumeration	44 ⊕	54	↓	⌁	
Detection	17 ⊕	18	→	⌁	
Management	29 !⊕	27	→	⌁	

Overall risk

Show last
8 quarters

Target

July '13   July '14   July '15

↑ Significant increase since last report
→ No change since last report
↓ Significant decrease since last report

⊕ Precision / accuracy
! Critical risk issue needs to be addressed

EXHIBIT 10.2. This exhibit contains top-level financial metrics and risk indicators for the Owner as stakeholder. Arrows denote significant movement since the previous report, trend charts are available for all measures. The icon ⊕ contains information about precision and accuracy of the performance metric. The alert (!) denotes a critical risk issue that arose at a lower level, and is forced to persist to the top level of reporting. The chart icon ⌁ (dark when selected) is used to view a chart.

issue is being managed. The electronic nature of the report facilitates access to a short report (Exhibit 10.4(a)) to provide further explanation. This indicator is reserved for a mission-critical risk. It may have been detected at quite a low level in the enterprise, but is so serious that it must be drawn to the Board's attention, so it

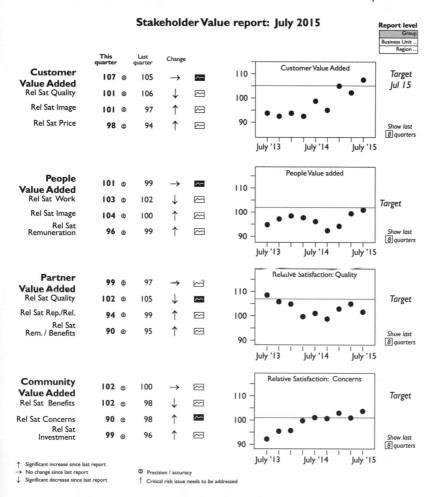

Stakeholder Value report: July 2015

EXHIBIT 10.3. This exhibit complements Exhibit 10.2, by providing the top-level measures for the other stakeholder groups. All scores are relative to 100 (par with the competition). The icon ⊕ contains information about precision and accuracy of the performance metric. (For such relative value scores, the precision is typically ± 2). Each relative value score has three drivers. Collectively, they capture the current position with all stakeholders (they are lag indicators).

cannot be erased from the system except at Board level – the warning must persist in all higher level reports.

Stakeholder Value metrics (Exhibit 10.3). This exhibit contains the high-level information about how the enterprise is managing its relationships with its other key stakeholders. All scores are benchmarked so that the value 100 represents a par score.

The scores are obtained by aggregating scores over all Business Units, weighting the results for each Business Unit by the relative

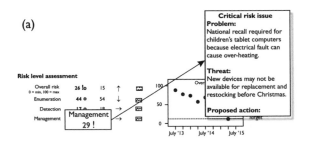

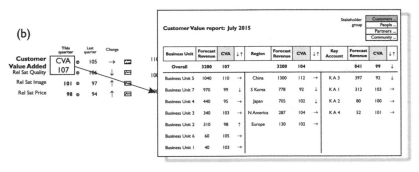

EXHIBIT 10.4. Lower-level reports associated with the top-level Group report in Exhibit 10.2, providing the capability to drill down to explore issues arising from the top-level report. (a) The Risk Management alert in Exhibit 10.2 has an associated note providing relevant details. (b) In the detailed Customer Value report, Forecast revenue = yearly planned revenue. Overall CVA is the average over all Business Unit (or Region) CVAs weighted by Forecast revenues. The high Customer Value Added score in Exhibit 10.3 can be studied in more detail by looking at an associated report, showing CVA scores by Business Unit, Region or Key Account.

proportion of its planned revenue for the year. From this, we can observe that:

- The enterprise has performed strongly in the marketplace over the last year and is in a dominant position despite a drop overall in perceived Quality, relative to the competition. Exhibit 10.4(b) reveals greater detail about where the excellent performance is occurring.
- An improved performance with People over the last year has the enterprise close to its target, which was slightly above par.
- Relationships with Partners are consistently below the target the enterprise had set for itself, and some sort of specific intervention might be required.
- A committed two-year effort to improving the relationship with the Community appears to have worked well.

Associated with this top-level report are numerous optional lower-level reports and summaries that enable probing of specific issues. In particular, there is an important accompaniment to reports at the Business Unit or Regional level: *Brief explanatory reports by the responsible senior officer.* In the context of managing Customer Value, Ray Kordupleski comments:[8]

> The very best reports I've seen contain a one-page analysis of each business unit's results, written and signed by the senior officer responsible for that business unit. The comment gives the President's or managing director's view on why the results are what they are, what's behind the trends and what the business unit is going to do to improve or sustain the scores. It may also include some analysis of key competitors in that market – their strengths and weaknesses, their strategy, the company's response.
>
> In my view, it's critical that these commentaries not be written by market researchers or the customer value team. While these staff people will no doubt influence the president's views, it is the senior officer who's responsible. He or she must take accountability for the scores and commit to action.

Also available at the Business Unit level would be the sorts of top-level Value reports and associated graphs we saw in earlier chapters (*e.g.* Exhibits 5.5 and 5.8).

Reports that answer the question: "Where are we heading?"

Complementing the previous set of reports, another set is needed that indicates where the enterprise is heading and where attention must be directed, specifically. That is, how should priorities for action be chosen to have the best impact on the business?

To identify this set of metrics, we return to the Board Value tree. Exhibit 10.1 shows that six sets of indicators are needed, relating to:

a. Returns
b. Annual Business Cycle
c. Wellness
d. Risk Enumeration
e. Risk Detection
f. Risk Management.

Exhibit 10.5 provides some suggestions about the sorts of lead indictors that might be used for our retail sector example. Of course, the reporting format for these will be similar to what was used for lag indictors, as exemplified in Exhibits 10.6 and 10.7 for some of the indicators.

It is important to realize that suitable lead indicators may not be easy to identify, particularly in relation to some Attributes of Returns and Risk that are very much industry-dependent. We have identified *Unemployment* and *Consumer sentiment* as helpful indicators for Profitability – for the retail sector. If we take a very different business, such as a pulp-milling plant, these indicators would be replaced by quite different economic indicators, such as trends in the supply of paper for printing purposes (likely to be decreasing with time) and trends in the tissue market (likely to increase). The important thing is to identify meaningful indictors – *i.e.* indicators with genuine predictive capability, difficult though it may be. The more light you can shine in the direction you're heading the better.

EXHIBIT 10.5. Examples of possible lead indicators.

	Lag indicators	Lead indicators
Returns	Profitability	
	EBIT	Unemployment rate
	Return on Equity	Consumer sentiment
	Gross Profit margin	Increase/decrease in # of stores
	Sales per store	Market share
	...	Customer loyalty
		Unplanned staff turnover
		Community support
	Solvency	
	Current ratio	Cash flow forecast
	Net debt/equity	Debtor days
		Interest cover
	Financial flexibility	
	Lines of credit	Cash flow forecast
	Interest cover	...
	Debt maturities	...
	Asset-holding Risk	
	Stock markdowns	Age of inventory
	...	...
How generated	Confirm business model	# unforeseen adjustments
	Plan the year's work	% critical deadlines achieved
	Carry out the work	% improvement targets achieved
	Evaluate the results	% objectives achieved
Wellness	CVA	Customer Value
	PVA	People Value
	PartnerVA	Partner Value
	CommunityVA	Community Value
	Agency rating	...
	Quality of Assets	...
Risk	Enumeration Risk score (0–100)	# Class One events
		% complete/ incident-free audits
	Detection score (0–100)	% compliance w/statutory reporting
	Management score (0–100)	# unplanned loss of key staff
		# unplanned loss of major client

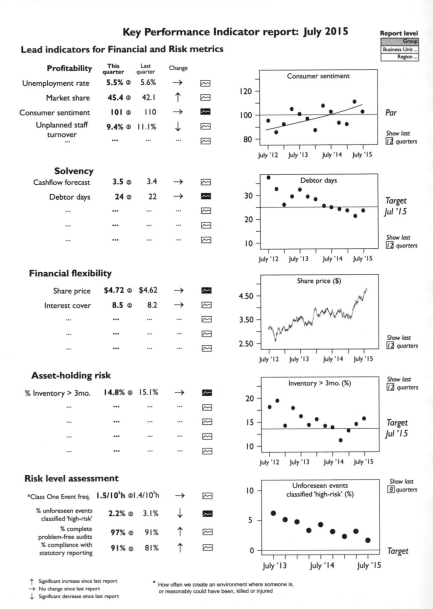

Key Performance Indicator report: July 2015

Report level
Group
Business Unit ...
Region ...

Lead indicators for Financial and Risk metrics

Profitability	This quarter	Last quarter	Change		
Unemployment rate	**5.5%** ⊕	5.6%	→	≈	
Market share	**45.4** ⊕	42.1	↑	≈	
Consumer sentiment	**101** ⊕	110	→	≈	
Unplanned staff turnover	**9.4%** ⊕	11.1%	↓	≈	
...	...	...	...	≈	

Consumer sentiment — Par — Show last 12 quarters

Solvency

Cashflow forecast	**3.5** ⊕	3.4	→	≈	
Debtor days	**24** ⊕	22	→	≈	
...	...	...	...	≈	
...	...	...	...	≈	
...	...	...	...	≈	

Debtor days — Target Jul '15 — Show last 12 quarters

Financial flexibility

Share price	**$4.72** ⊕	$4.62	→	≈	
Interest cover	**8.5** ⊕	8.2	→	≈	
...	...	...	...	≈	
...	...	...	...	≈	
...	...	...	...	≈	

Share price ($) — Show last 12 quarters

Asset-holding risk

% Inventory > 3mo.	**14.8%** ⊕	15.1%	→	≈	
...	...	...	...	≈	
...	...	...	...	≈	
...	...	...	...	≈	
...	...	...	...	≈	

Inventory > 3mo. (%) — Show last 12 quarters — Target Jul '15

Risk level assessment

*Class One Event freq.	**1.5/10⁵h** ⊕	1.4/10⁵h	→	≈	
% unforeseen events classified 'high-risk'	**2.2%** ⊕	3.1%	↓	≈	
% complete problem-free audits	**97%** ⊕	91%	↑	≈	
% compliance with statutory reporting	**91%** ⊕	81%	↑	≈	

Unforeseen events classified 'high-risk' (%) — Show last 8 quarters — Target

↑ Significant increase since last report
→ No change since last report
↓ Significant decrease since last report

* How often we create an environment where someone is, or reasonably could have been, killed or injured

EXHIBIT 10.6. Some lead Financial and Risk indicators, to help predict where the enterprise is heading, to enable the leadership to take action in anticipation of problems, and also to capitalize on emerging opportunities. Note how trends in individual graphs in Exhibit 10.6 anticipate corresponding trends in Exhibit 10.2. The indicators relate to the financial and risk management aspects of the business.

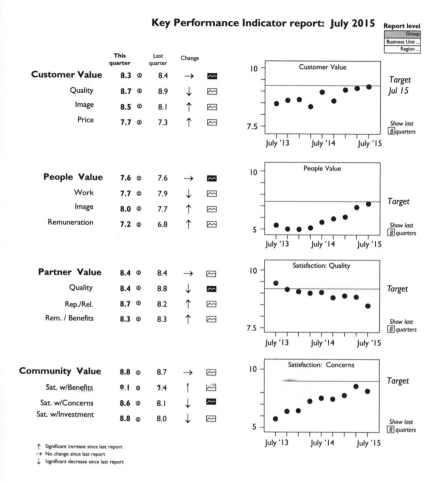

EXHIBIT 10.7. Lead indicators for the other stakeholder groups. All scores are ratings on the scale (Poor) to 10 (Excellent). They are the current ratings for your enterprise, whereas those in Exhibit 10.3 are measured relative to your competitors.

Sometimes reports in the form of tables will be adequate. However, graphs need to be used if the indicators have interesting patterns of behavior.

For example, suppose each Division of your company has run an initial survey assessing people's confidence in their manager's approach to Safety. "Confidence" has been measured on a 10-point scale, where 1 = Total lack of Confidence and 10 = Fully Confident.

Based on benchmarking considerations with similar companies, your initial target is an overall average of 8.2. However, you realize that the cultures and conditions of your ten Business Units are very different, so you ask for the data to be reported as an overall summary and by Business Unit. Just as well you did! See Exhibit 10.8: one of the Business Units is lagging behind.

10.3   PRESENTING THE INITIAL REPORTS:
THE PLANNING WORKSHOP

Why did Ray Kordupleski devote a whole chapter of his book on managing Customer Value to this issue?[9]

> All the time and money spent capturing and analysing the data and helping people understand and accept it is wasted if it doesn't lead to action. So the workshop design I use actually gets people picking priorities and building action plans ...
>
> In my mind these experiential workshops are the make-or-break point in your customer value journey. If you can't get your senior people to engage with the data and start using it to pick priorities you're in for a hard slog to embed customer value management into the business. If you skip this step altogether, I can guarantee you won't get maximum return on your data collection investment.

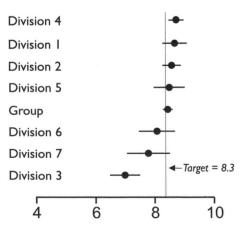

Confidence intervals for mean Safety ratings

EXHIBIT 10.8. Mean Safety ratings for seven Divisions and for the overall group, together with estimates of precision. Whilst the overall Group average has reached the target value of 8.3, one Division lags well behind (its confidence interval does not include the target).

We'll describe the details of the workshop in Section 12.6. The three overall steps outlined by Kordupleski, and equally applicable here, are:

1. to create understanding of the value concepts and tools;
2. to gain acceptance of the results by participants; and
3. to develop an action plan.

The real deliverable is the workshop and its outcomes, not the reports.

10.4   CODA: CONNECTIONS BETWEEN LEAD AND LAG INDICATORS

While we've stressed the importance of lead indicators as predictors of future performance, we haven't said much about exhibiting this. The examples in Exhibit 1.7 (*People Value* score as a lead indicator for reduction in *Unplanned staff turnover*) and Exhibit 5.3 (*Customer Value* as a lead indicator for *Market Share*) exemplify the sort of relationship to seek. The key to identifying and exploiting such relationships is to accumulate data on an ongoing basis, and then carry out the appropriate statistical analysis. Other such high-level links might include *Community Value* as a lead indicator of Community support for a proposed government action.

In their discussion of the Sears Employee–Customer–Profit chain, Rucci, Kirn and Quinn (1998) make the point that

> Making an employee–customer–profit chain operational is ... a challenge in three parts: creating and refining the employee–customer–profit model and the measurement system that supports it; creating management alignment around the use of the model to run the company; and deploying the model so as to build business literacy and trust among employees.[10]

The second and third of these points are intrinsic to the whole Value management process as originally realized by Kordupleski in his approach to managing Customer Value. We would argue that the first point is part of a broader (and significantly statistical) modeling issue, as it needs to accommodate Partners and the Community as well. This is an important area for future research.

Of course, there are lower-level linkages to establish as well. For example:

- the operational metrics shown in Exhibit 5.11 that are put in place to track performance with customer requirements such as *Responsiveness, Promises Kept, Knowledgeable people, etc.*
- cross-relating the rating of *Training and development appropriate to my job*, or even *Work Environment*, from a People Value survey, to the rating of *Knowledgeable people* in a Customer Value survey.

The following case study from AT&T illustrates the importance of understanding and monitoring the connection between metrics associated with various stakeholder groups:

> AT&T had a firm commitment to a balanced scorecard approach and placed significant goals and compensation rewards for meeting increasing levels of customer satisfaction and employee satisfaction. But in this particular case, increasing levels of employee satisfaction with sales employees was the cause for decreasing levels of customer satisfaction with sales support and also decreasing sales revenue.
>
> The background to this was that the human resource department recognized that young MBA graduates were very willing to take an entry level job in sales to start their career with AT&T. Management wanted to take the opportunity to hire these highly qualified people and give them the benefit of learning the business from the sales and marketing perspective.
>
> Quickly though, these upwardly mobile employees became dissatisfied with just a typical sales job and employee satisfaction in the sales department dropped. To improve the employee satisfaction scores management needed to rotate the sales force territory frequently and to also provide non-sales jobs so that these employees felt that their growth and development needs were being

cared for. These changes worked well and employee satisfaction rose significantly.

At the same time however, customer satisfaction with sales deteriorated which lowered the perceived value of the services received and customer retention dropped as did market share because customer satisfaction with sales was a 30% driver of overall quality and a 15% driver of overall value.

Root cause analysis determined that the biggest driver of customer satisfaction with sales was the relationship a sales person had with the customer. With a little investigation it was easy to determine that the young sales people did a great job establishing a relationship, but a poor job of maintaining one. Direct input from key account customers clearly said such things as "We'd just got the sales person trained about our business and our needs only to have him or her transferred and a new person assigned. And this is happening frequently and across our territories."

Not only did customer satisfaction suffer, but so did revenue because of defections and losses to the competition.

Customers wanted sales people who wanted to be sales people. They wanted sales people who wanted to live and stay in and be part of the community their business was. They wanted people who were interested in their business growth and development and not people who were more interested in their own growth and development and viewed a sales job as a learning experience.

It was not until HR changed its hiring policies to match the desires of the customer to the skills and desires of the people they put into sales that the employee and customer satisfaction scores improved and the market share and revenue improved also.

Ray Kordupleski, personal communication

NOTES

1 A fragment of an unknown tragedy by Euripides, in *The nineteen tragedies and fragments of Euripides*, 3 volumes, translated by

Michael Wodhull, 1809, Volume 3, page 414, line B268, General Books: London.

2 Ray Kordupleski (personal communication) offered the following reminiscence from his AT&T days: "The old saying goes, 'timing is everything'. In the case of the stakeholder reports, 'time is of the essence'. Bob Allen, when he was the Chairman of AT&T was very astute and precise in his directives about the timing of the Customer Value reports. The quarterly board meeting date set the drum beat to which the sequence of all reports and preparations for the quarterly meeting took place. The Board meetings were set for the third Wednesday of every quarter. At those meetings major decisions were made and the Customer data were integral to the decisions. The customer data were considered as important as the financials and therefore their completion and distribution had to be in absolute sync with the distribution of the financial data to the fiduciary officers and the board of directors. Mr. Allen knew if the Customer Reports were not in sync with the financial reports they provided little value since most decisions would already have been made. Timing is especially critical during the annual business planning cycle when goals are set, resources are committed and officers sign their name to annual commitments."

3 Reproduced from Section 1.2 with additional explanation.

4 They are organized under the four basic headings of Profitability, Solvency, Financial flexibility and Asset-holding risk advocated, for example, in Chambers (1986); however, the organization is simply a matter of personal preference.

5 Precision versus Accuracy: what's the difference?

Precision refers to the amount of *uncertainty* associated with an indicator, if appropriate. For example, is the Customer Value indicator reliable to within ± 2% or ± 10%?

Accuracy refers to any potential source of *bias*. For example, does the estimate of overall market share exclude any markets? (Chatterji and Levine (2006) comment: "To be blunt, because many surveys have response rates below 20 percent, we cannot be sure about the accuracy of many non-financial performance metrics.")

Precision and *accuracy* are complementary notions, as shown in Exhibit 10.9.

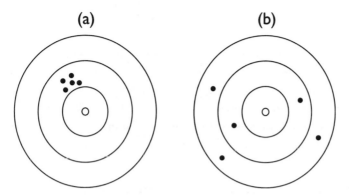

EXHIBIT 10.9. Distinguishing between Precision and Accuracy. (a) Precision: the shots at the target are concentrated, but not around the bulls-eye. The position of the next shot can be forecast with some reasonable degree of precision. (b) Accuracy: the shots fall around the bulls-eye, but are so variable that predicting where the next one will fall cannot be done with any degree of confidence.

6 There is a vast literature on Risk Management, and there are numerous approaches to the topic. A simple process is described, for example, at www.business.qld.gov.au/business/running/risk-management/pprr-risk-management model.

Kaplan and Mikes (2012) describe another approach linked to formulation of strategy and implementation processes:

"To some extent, the approach you select is a matter of taste. The reporting system requires that the approach produce metrics that can provide a comprehensive assessment of risk, so that the appropriate people are alerted in as timely a fashion as possible."

7 The article by Tinsley, Dillon and Madsen (2011) is also interesting in this regard. To quote from the Abstract:

"Most business failures such as engineering disasters, product malfunctions, and PR crises are foreshadowed by near misses, close calls that, had luck not intervened, would have had far worse consequences. The space shuttle Columbia's fatal re-entry, BP's Gulf oil rig disaster, Toyota's stuck accelerators, even the iPhone 4's antenna failures – all were preceded by near-miss events that should have tipped off managers to impending crises. The problem is that near misses are often overlooked – or, perversely, viewed as a sign that systems are resilient and working well. That's because managers are blinded by cognitive biases...

"Seven strategies can help managers recognize and learn from near misses: They should be on increased alert when time or cost pressures are high; watch for deviations in operations from the norm and uncover their root causes; make decision makers accountable for near misses; envision worst-case scenarios; be on the lookout for near-misses masquerading as successes; and reward individuals for exposing near misses."

8 Kordupleski (2003), page 172.
9 *Ibid.* Chapter 11. The quoted passage is from pages 204–5.
10 Rucci *et al.* (1998), page 84.

11 How to get started ...

Knowledge without know-how is sterile.

Myron Tribus

11.1 PREAMBLE: WHERE ARE WE NOW?

How are data and information currently being used throughout your enterprise to:

- manage risk?
- inform decision-making – getting the right information, at the right time, in actionable format?
- improve all aspects of the business – using business analytics, Six Sigma *etc.*?

The best entrée to adopting the performance measurement system described in earlier chapters is to find out the answers to these questions. *And this is not a major undertaking*: It can be accomplished in days not weeks, and by just a small team of two people, with only modest demands on management time.

The outcome of the assessment process will be a list of prioritized improvement strategies and action plans, developed with the leadership, that form the basis for getting started.

11.2 THE PERFORMANCE MEASUREMENT FRAMEWORK ASSESSMENT PROCESS

The goal is to assess the status of the enterprise against eight basic criteria[1] (see Exhibit 11.1) relating to the Performance Measurement Framework, as a basis for improvement.

Here we give an overview of the assessment process, with the details deferred to Chapter 12. It is modeled on a proven process developed by Norbert Vogel, a leading practitioner in devising and

EXHIBIT 11.1. Criteria used in an initial assessment of an enterprise against the Performance Measurement Framework, and the areas explored for each criterion.

Criterion	Issues discussed
1. Strategic measurement	1.1 Identification of main stakeholder groups
	1.2 Identification of stakeholder needs and expectations
	1.3 Measurement of outcomes delivered to stakeholders
2. Tactical measurement	2.1 Identification of measures
	2.2 Use of measures
3. Operational measurement	3.1 Identification of processes
	3.2 Measurement of processes and their outputs
4. Role Alignment	4.1 Accountability, Responsibility and Authority
	4.2 Performance management
5. Scope of data	5.1 Stakeholder Value
	5.2 Process and Output measures
6. Data collection processes	6.1 Data collection
	6.2 Data integrity
7. Data analysis and use	7.1 Interpretation of data
	7.2 Analysis of data
8. Ongoing review of the measurement system	8.1 Review process

deploying methodologies for evaluating enterprises against Business Excellence frameworks.

The assessment process involves the collection of information to provide a snapshot of how effectively the organization addresses the criteria listed above. Information is sourced in a number of ways, including plans, observations on work practices, relevant reports and verbal responses to questions put to a cross-section of stakeholders identified prior to the start of an assessment visit.

Many audit and assessment processes require the organization to prepare a lot of specific documentation prior to the assessment visit but the need for separate documentation should be minimized. It is important that the assessment team acquires an understanding of the organizational profile prior to the assessment visit to enable questions to be framed in an appropriate context. Such information includes an understanding of the organization's governance structure, its key stakeholders, the competitive and business environment in which it operates, its resources and its core products and services. Usually, much of this information can be obtained from the organization's web site and its most recent annual report.

In preparation for an assessment, the organization is requested to make available relevant documents for the assessment team to examine during the visit. These include planning documents, relevant policies, performance reports, minutes of Board and management meetings, relevant Terms of Reference and protocols and communication documents. Such materials provide information on what is actually happening, which is often not the case with documents specifically prepared for an assessment. Examination of these documents is primarily used to gain an understanding of the organization's "Approach" to each of the criteria. That is, "How do you do this or how do you plan to do this?"

The effectiveness of the "Approach" is best determined through discussions with a cross-section of stakeholders, including staff, Board members, clients, partners and investors. So, advance preparations include identifying appropriate people to interview and arranging an interview schedule. An assessment visit would generally take place over three or four consecutive days for a single-site enterprise.

After the visit, the team prepares a draft report that evaluates the organization's performance against each criterion; a commentary on the team's findings for that criterion and suggestions about Strengths and Opportunities for Improvement. This report is checked for factual errors with the leader, and then provided to participants in the planning workshop a couple of days in advance.

The deliverable is a prioritized list of improvement strategies and action plans. The team facilitates a workshop process in which participants evaluate the various opportunities identified in the report, formulate recommendations in response to these opportunities, allocate priorities, and identify the next steps.

In other words, the recommendations are developed, prioritized and owned by the enterprise itself. They are not handed down by the evaluation team, Moses-style on stone tablets. As we shall see, adoption of a stakeholder management process follows very similar lines.

Evaluation of an enterprise against the Performance Measurement Framework differs from a more general evaluation against Business Excellence criteria in one important way: here, the principle of Alignment dictates that the recommendations relating to the *Strategic Measurement* and *Tactical Measurement* criteria need to be addressed before others are tackled. For example, little progress can be made in the absence of a sound stakeholder analysis.

Chapter 13 contains detailed information about conducting an assessment against the Performance Measurement Framework.

11.3   GETTING STARTED WITH STAKEHOLDER VALUE MANAGEMENT

This presupposes that you have indeed identified your various stakeholders! Otherwise, you'll need to conduct a Stakeholder Analysis. At a minimum, the Stakeholder Analysis needs to identify all the different groups which need to be considered, together with any information that might provide the basis for deciding on their relative importance. One such example for a large hospital run by a religious order is shown in Exhibit 11.2. Of course, much, if not all, of this information will be resident in your Strategic Plan.

In terms of learning how to operate the Value Analysis process, it is easiest to start either with Customers or with People.

EXHIBIT 11.2. Output of a Stakeholder Analysis for a hospital run by a religious order. The priorities identified here, plus other strategic considerations, help to identify where to target Stakeholder Value initiatives.

Stakeholder group	Key current issues	Priority
1. Owners:	1.1 Evidence of Mission inculcated throughout organization	2
	1.2 Services for the marginalized	4
2. Customers:		
Patients	2.1 Communication regarding care	1
	2.2 Perception of safety and support	1
Families and carers	2.3 Communication regarding their involvement in care	1
	2.4 Availability of family facilities	3
	2.5 Involvement in care	3
3. People:		
Doctors	3.1 Standard of physical facilities	2
Nursing staff	3.2 Patient satisfaction	2
Non-medical	3.3 Financial rewards	2
staff	3.4 Physical labor required by the job	1
4. Strategic Partners:		
Insurance funds	4.1 Clinical outcomes for contributors	3
Visiting medical officers	4.2 Standard of physical facilities	2
Referring doctors	4.3 Clinical outcomes for contributors	3
5. Community:		
Local	5.1 Contribution to community activities	2
Other hospitals	5.2 Overflow bed arrangements	1

For the Customer market, the selection of which particular market to tackle will usually be settled by the revenue delivered to your business by that market and strategic considerations.

Then it's a matter of working with a Customer Value expert whose role it is to:

- explain the Value Analysis process to the leadership team;
- work with you to develop the survey instrument, test it and deploy it;
- analyze the initial data and prepare a report; and
- present the results in the form of a workshop.

The importance of the (half-day) workshop[2] cannot be over-emphasized. Several important actions take place:

- *Your team develops an understanding of what the results mean.* After all, you'll be seeing the same sorts of reports (whether for Customers or People *etc.*) on a regular basis and don't want to have to re-learn what it all means every time. That's part of the beauty of the system: Value Analysis reports can all be interpreted and acted on in the same way, regardless of the stakeholder or the market.
- *You make preliminary identification of improvement priorities.* This will be based on Root Cause analysis and other basic quality improvement tools that can be used in the workshop to see where problems originate.
- *You commission teams to address the priorities.* This may involve the need to develop internal skills and capabilities (*e.g.* Six Sigma) to carry out the improvements.
- You communicate the results of the workshop to the people in your enterprise.

And then the basic cycle in Exhibit 4.2 takes over – make the improvements, communicate them to the market and re-survey.

Details about implementing stakeholder management processes are provided in Chapter 13.

11.4   REQUIREMENTS FOR ENTERPRISE CAPABILITY

One area that hasn't been addressed in this book is that of the capability required within the enterprise to introduce a performance measurement system. On this subject, comments made by Robert Eccles in 1991 remain true to this day:

The leading indicators of business performance cannot be found in financial data alone. Quality, customer satisfaction, innovation, market share – metrics like these often reflect a company's economic condition and growth prospects better than its reported earnings do. Depending on an accounting department to reveal a company's future will leave it hopelessly mired in the past.

More and more managers are changing their company's performance measurement systems to track nonfinancial measures and reinforce competitive strategies. Five activities are essential: developing an information architecture; putting the technology in place to support this architecture; aligning bonuses and other incentives with the new system; drawing on outside resources; and designing an internal process to ensure the other four activities occur...

Every company will have its own key measures and distinctive process for implementing the change. But making it happen will always require careful preparation, perseverance, and the conviction of the CEO that it must be carried through.[3]

NOTES

1 These criteria were devised by a CSIRO team involved in implementing the OPM (Organizational Performance Measurement) methodology from which the Performance Measurement Framework is derived.
2 Kordupleski (2003) provides a lot of advice about responding to Customer Value reports.
3 Eccles (1991).

12 The Performance Measurement Framework: Assessment and adoption

12.1 PREAMBLE: AN ASSESSMENT, NOT AN AUDIT

Remember our overall goal as stated in Exhibit 2.1 in Chapter 2: we aimed to describe a system for performance measurement that provides:

1. a concise overview of health of your enterprise;
2. a quantitative basis for selecting improvement priorities; and
3. alignment of the efforts of the people with the mission of the enterprise.

The purpose of an assessment (*cf.* Section 11.2) is to evaluate how well your current approach to performance measurement is helping you achieve this. The assessment is based on the eight criteria described in Exhibit 11.1 and also depicted in Exhibit 12.1, which derive from the Performance Measurement Framework.

The approach to performing the assessment is essentially based on the approach used for Business Excellence frameworks such as that of the Baldrige or the European Foundation for Quality Management (EFQM). Each criterion is evaluated in terms of

> Approach: the extent to which appropriate systems, processes, procedures and structures are in place to make it possible to satisfy the criterion;

and

> Deployment: the extent to which the systems, processes, procedures and structures are being applied as intended.

It is important to recognize the difference between an *assessment* process of the type proposed below, and a *compliance audit* process. Exhibit 12.2, due to Norbert Vogel, sets out the differences

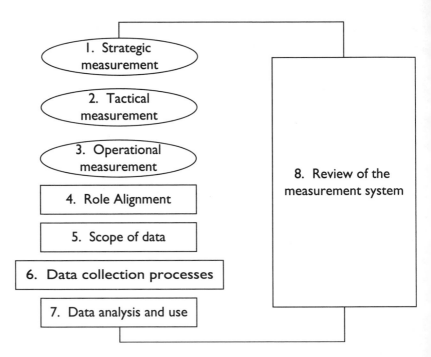

EXHIBIT 12.1. Criteria used in conducting an assessment of the enterprise against the Performance Measurement Framework.

in the context of Business Excellence frameworks, but similar considerations apply here.

12.2   ASSESSMENT PROCESS STEPS

One form of evaluation process that has been shown to work well is as follows:

Prior to the assessment visit

Step 1   The assessment team familiarizes itself with the organizational profile as outlined in the previous chapter. A schedule of interviews with a cross-section of staff and other key stakeholders is prepared in conjunction with the organization, together with arrangements for access to key documents to be reviewed by the assessment team. Also, schedule a half-day planning workshop about four weeks after the visit to allow sufficient time for preparation and distribution of the report prior to the workshop.

EXHIBIT 12.2. Norbert Vogel's comparison of Accreditation Audits and Business Excellence Evaluations.

Characteristic	Accreditation Audit	Excellence Evaluation
Definition	A process by which compliance with a standard or set of rules and requirements is verified	A process that examines how effectively non-prescriptive criteria or guidelines are addressed and implemented
Primary focus	Compliance	Improvement of organizational performance and capability
Primary activity	Validation of information provided through a process of internal audit	Analysis and evaluation of information collected by the evaluation team
Description of criteria	Rules-based, prescriptive, binary	Options-based, non-prescriptive, non-binary
Prevalent form of questioning	Closed	Open
Documentation of findings	Level of compliance with stated requirements and identification of non-compliances	Identification of strengths and opportunities for improvement
Scope of review	Operational activities	Degree of effectiveness
Predominant focus	Operational activities	Broader organizational capabilities and performance
Form of recognition	Certificate of compliance	Recognition of intent to pursue business improvement towards achievement of outstanding performance

Step 2   A few days beforehand, request that a room be made available on arrival, with a number of currently existing documents provided for review (in other words, nothing should be prepared specially, for this purpose). (See Section 11.2 for suggestions about relevant documents.)

The assessment team review and make notes about these materials during their visit, but do not remove the materials.

The assessment visit

Step 3   Conduct the visit, carrying out the scheduled interviews and reviewing the documents provided. See Section 12.3 for a discussion of this data-gathering phase.

Prior to the planning workshop

Step 4   After the visit, analyze the qualitative and quantitative data, prepare a draft report that evaluates the organization's performance against each criterion. This comprises a commentary on the team's findings for that criterion and suggestions about:

- Strengths (*e.g.* demonstrable deployment of the use of graphs where appropriate, to report quantitative information);
- Opportunities for Improvement – the nature of the opportunity, but not how to address it (*e.g.* strengthen the market segmentation and prioritization for the Customer market, but not how to carry this out).

Step 5   Send the draft report to the senior officer about a week before the planning workshop, with an invitation to point out errors of fact or of major concern. Advise the officer that it is classified as a draft, and request that it not be circulated to anyone else.

Step 6   Make any final changes required, and send a copy for distribution to workshop attendees in time for them to read it in advance (2–3 days before the workshop). It is worth emphasizing that the report is intended to be used as an internal working document for the management team to use as a reference for determining a prioritized list of improvement strategies. It is *not* intended for wider distribution. Providing it to planning workshop participants beforehand allows them to prepare better for the session, with "no surprises."

Step 7   Prepare some material for distribution as hard copy *at* the workshop:

a. A worksheet in the form of a table listing the opportunities for improvement, grouped by Criterion; see Exhibit 12.3.

b. A list of the Strengths, for distribution to everyone in the organization, to let them know what the assessment team believes is being done well.

The planning workshop

Step 8   Facilitate discussion about improvement opportunities:

      a. Individuals classify each opportunity according to Importance and Urgency.

      b. Discuss classification and record consensus on white board or large chart, as shown in Exhibit 12.4.

      c. Discuss which ones are linked – *e.g.* 1.1, 2.1 and 2.2 in Exhibit 11.2.

      d. Develop set of prioritized recommendations

Step 9   Discuss communication of the recommendations to everyone in the enterprise. A summary communiqué that lists high-level findings of strengths and prioritized improvement strategies determined by the management team is the most effective way of communicating with staff and others who participated in interviews.

After the planning workshop

Step 10   Update the report with the agreed recommendations, and send final report to leader.

EXHIBIT 12.3. Chart for recording agreed priorities for the improvement opportunities. The principle relating to Alignment means that some opportunities need to be addressed before others. Of course, other factors will also affect the assignment of priorities.

		Importance		
		Low	Medium	High
	Low	*etc.*	*etc.*	1.1.1
				1.2.1
				1.2.2
				...
Urgency	Medium	*etc.*	*etc.*	1.3.1
				1.3.2
				...
	High	*etc.*	*etc.*	*etc.*

EXHIBIT 12.4. Worksheet for workshop participants to record their initial allocation of priorities for the improvement opportunities.

Criterion	Improvement opportunity	Initial priority* U	I
1. Strategic Mst.			
1.1 Identify main stakeholder groups	1.1.1 Clarify distinct Customer and Community stakeholder groups		
1.2 Identify stakeholder needs and expectations	1.2.1 Develop priorities for the distinct Customer and Community stakeholder groups identified in item 1.1.1		
	1.2.2 Develop provisional Value trees for People, Partners, Owners, and for groups identified as high priority in 1.2.1		
1.3 Measure outcomes delivered to stakeholders	1.3.1 Develop priorities for implementing Value Management processes for the groups identified in item 1.2.2		
	1.3.2 Implement Stakeholder Value processes based on item 1.3.1		
2. Tactical Mst.			
2.1 Identification of measures	2.1.1 ...		
etc.	etc.		

*Note: The use of relative Urgency (U) and Importance (I) is really just a first cut for prioritization. Other considerations for determining actual priorities and action plans should also include ease of implementation, cost, resources required, as well as cause–effect relationships that require certain opportunities to be addressed prior to others. Urgency and Importance are scored as in Exhibit 12.3.

12.3   CONDUCTING THE INTERVIEWS

This aspect of the process will be familiar to anyone who has been involved in evaluations against Business Excellence criteria such as Baldrige, EFQM or McKinsey 7S. You're seeking to elicit information about the enterprise's practices under each of the eight criteria in Exhibit 11.1 by asking open-ended questions. Listed below are some specific issues that can be queried in relation to each criterion.[1] The sorts of conversation-openers that have proven to be helpful in many such assessments are questions like "What is your job?" and "How do you know you are doing a good job?"

Responses to these questions lead naturally into developing an appreciation of the way people think about their work. (Have they got a stakeholder focus, even if it is simply on their internal customer? Do they understand the scope of their job, *i.e.* their areas of Accountability? Do they appreciate the difference between their areas of Accountability and areas of Responsibility? What sorts of data do they think they need to do their job well? And so on.)

Of course, the emphasis put on covering each criterion will necessarily vary according to the role of each individual in the enterprise.

Strategic measurement

The focus here is on assessing how well the enterprise understands

- stakeholders and their needs
- current and planned performance relative to stakeholder needs.

In this regard, strategic measures, or *Success Measures*, need to

- quantify the overall achievement of the organization in adding value for each stakeholder group
- capture an external assessment of performance against desirable outcomes
- provide a comparative assessment of performance.

The basic concepts being explored are stakeholders and the definition of Stakeholder Value.

Questions and considerations

- Who are the major stakeholder groups?
- What are their needs?
- Identification of major stakeholders and their requirements in organizational documents, such as the Strategic Plan.
- What does "Success" mean for the organization's stakeholders?
- Identification of the key drivers of stakeholder satisfaction for the main stakeholder groups.
- Monitoring of stakeholder views, and use of this information to determine priorities for improvement.
- How the competing needs of different stakeholders are managed.
- Do the Mission and Vision reflect the stakeholder needs and are they expressed in a way that facilitates measurement of progress?

Tactical measurement

Success Measures tell the enterprise whether competitive value has been delivered to stakeholders, whereas KPIs tell the enterprise whether it is *likely* to be delivered. KPIs reflect the major outputs that the organization must deliver and, collectively, represent the functioning of the enterprise as a whole.

The basic concepts to be explored are:

- alignment of KPIs with the strategic intent of the organization
- alignment of KPIs with the stakeholders' needs and core business processes
- clear, timely and actionable reporting of KPIs
- use of KPIs to inform leadership and management action.

Questions and considerations

- What sorts of measures (Success Measures, KPIs or other) are associated with any organizational plans and documents?
- Reporting of measures (format, frequency *etc.*) to the executive and management teams.
- The sorts of targets and goals associated with these organizational measures.

- How the Board and/or the executive team use the reported values of KPIs (or other measures) to determine how well the organization is performing.
- How this information is used to decide areas for organizational improvement.
- How the measures provide information on the effectiveness of the management system.
- How the measures relate to strategic plans or the strategic intent of the organization.
- How the measures relate to stakeholders' needs.

Operational measurement

The operational level of measurement includes measurements of the processes for product or service delivery. Process measures provide the basis for "real time" management at the operational level and enable

- control of processes, ensuring stability and predictability of output
- process improvement, improving the capability of the process.

Appropriate operational measures result from applying the Tribus Paradigm (see Section 3.3), leading to

- clarification of the outputs and outcomes required from a particular process, and how these will be measured
- an understanding of the processes that combine to produce the requisite outputs
- an understanding of what needs to be measured inside the process to monitor, control and improve the outputs.

The basic concepts to be explored are

- the relationship of process measures to the desired outputs of the process (cf. the Tribus Paradigm)
- alignment of operational measures with the desired outputs of the core processes.

Questions and considerations

- Understanding of the core enterprise-level processes.
- Understanding of the operational-level processes.
- Understanding of the relationship between operational processes and the core business processes and their major outputs; in other words, an appreciation of the contribution of the process to the organization's results.
- Documentation of processes, for example, by using flowcharts.
- Understanding of the quality requirements of the individual processes.
- How the quality requirements are measured.
- How process output measures are used to ensure conformance with the process quality requirements.
- How in-process measures are used to monitor, control and improve processes.

Role Alignment

Alignment is a fundamental principle of the Performance Measurement Framework. This principle extends to the role of an individual or team within the organization, and to the measurement of individual and/or team performance.

The Performance Measurement Framework distinguishes three levels of measurement: Strategic, Tactical and Operational, corresponding to Sarasohn's *Zones of Management*, with their associated processes for effective management at each level of the organization.

- The Strategic management processes are concerned with setting strategic direction, objectives and targets – the "future positioning" of the organization. These processes and the associated measures relate to enterprise effectiveness in terms of adding Value for all key stakeholder groups.

  The CEO of an organization would usually be the person accountable for this level of process.

- The Tactical processes are concerned with management effectiveness – the management of "internal capability." These processes relate to the alignment of the organization's work with the strategic objectives.

The senior executive team would usually be accountable for these processes, with individual executives taking individual Accountability for certain major functions (e.g. sales, human resources etc.).

- Operational management processes are concerned with the control and improvement of the processes that produce the "products and services" of the organization. These processes and the associated measures reflect operational effectiveness.

Front-line managers and staff are usually responsible for the management of these processes and their outputs.

The criterion of "Role Alignment" is concerned with

- appropriate allocation of Accountabilities (for specific outcomes) in accordance with the strategic direction and goals of the organization
- appropriate delegation of Responsibilities (for specific outputs) in accordance with the strategic direction and goals of the organization
- congruence between the outputs required of an individual or team and the processes that those particular individuals or teams manage.

From a measurement viewpoint, the role of an individual or of a team, and their ability to carry out that role, are closely related to the authority delegated to that person or team and their defined areas of accountability. Thus, alignment of measurement at an individual or team level with organizational purpose would also see a clear relationship between

- the processes a person (or team) is accountable for managing
- the delegated authority they have to manage these processes

- the measures used to assess the performance of the individual or team
- the outputs and outcomes that those processes produce.

Further, these would be aligned with the organization's strategic intent and reflected in

- goals and/or plans for teams and individuals
- job or position descriptions, performance agreements or contracts (*i.e.* these would include expected outputs and/or outcomes)
- processes for performance appraisal, performance review and planning and goal-setting
- team or individual reporting structures and processes
- the organization's reward and recognition system.

So, the basic concepts to be explored are

- Authority, Accountability and Responsibility
- process management
- clarification and articulation of intended outputs and outcomes at individual and team level
- reward and recognition system.

Questions and considerations
(In the following, the term "individual" refers to any person in the enterprise, from an operational person with no line management Responsibilities, to the most senior person.)

- How are roles clarified at the various levels of management throughout the organization:
  Strategic level
  Senior executive level
  Operational – manager and staff levels
  and to what extent do people know their roles?
- How is individual or team responsibility for processes made explicit?
- How are these roles defined in organizational documents?
- What is the basis for assessing each individual's performance?

- What measures are available to enable individual or team performance to be evaluated?
- To what extent are people aware of how their performance is measured and the reasons for doing so?
- Do the various staff and managers know how well they are performing?
- Are the measures aligned with the overall direction and goals of the organization?
- Are the measures consistent with the processes the individual/team manages?
- Are the measures consistent with the delegated Authority, Accountability and Responsibility of the individual or team? That is, do they have direct influence over the results that are achieved?
- Are there clear reporting and review mechanisms for individual and/or team performance?

Scope of data

The scope of data needed to manage an enterprise is broad. Information is required to inform management at all levels of the organization about the strategic processes, the tactical processes and the operational processes.

Some data will relate to the *external* environment, for example

- stakeholders' assessment of the performance of the enterprise,
- customer data – current and potential market information, customer segmentation and analysis, numbers and sizes of customers, market growth rate, demographics of current and potential markets *etc.*
- employment data
- supplier-related data
- political, economic, social, technological and other data capturing aspects of the external environment that can influence the performance of the enterprise.

Other, *internal*, data will relate to the capability of the enterprise to compete in each of its stakeholder markets, such as

- financial analysis (leverage, liquidity, activity and profitability ratios)
- cost drivers (staff costs, supply costs, overheads *etc.*)
- efficiency measures
- analysis of the cultural situation (staff surveys, Focus Group results *etc.*)
- self-assessment of organizational effectiveness
- HR measures (staff numbers, unplanned staff turnover, skills, training costs *etc.*)
- assessment of physical facilities (surveys, redevelopment costs *etc.*)
- industry benchmark data
- process measures at all levels of the enterprise
- survey data (market research, customer satisfaction surveys, staff surveys *etc.*).

So the basic concepts being explored are:

- competitive performance relative to stakeholder need (providing Stakeholder Value)
- external environmental data and information
- data regarding internal capability.

Questions and considerations
- Is the scope of data appropriate to the needs of the organization?
- Are the various markets well understood (size, needs *etc.*) and is this understanding supported with data?
- Are the stakeholder perceptions of Value understood for all stakeholders – customers, owners, staff, partners and community – and are these perceptions supported by data?
- Does the organization understand the drivers of Value for the stakeholders and is organizational performance in these areas quantified through measurement?

- How are these data analyzed and used to drive the strategic processes (evaluation and planning)?
- How is the performance of the organization benchmarked against that of competitors, for each stakeholder group?
- How is the performance of the organization's main functions described and quantified?
- How is the performance of the core processes (in terms of outputs) described, measured and reported?
- How is the performance of the operational functions described, measured and reported?
- How is the performance of the operational processes (in terms of outputs) described, measured and reported?

Data collection processes

Whereas "Scope of data" referred to the need for data, "data collection" includes those specifics that determine the integrity and accuracy of data, and, consequently, the value that the organization will derive from the data.

There are two basic organizational situations requiring data collection: management of the processes that produce the organization's products and services; and surveys of stakeholder perceptions.

Collecting data on processes, products and services

This immediately raises issues[2] relating to *operational definitions*:

a. How is a particular measurement to be specified?
b. How is the measurement to be made?
c. How will the data be recorded and stored?

Each of these requires an explanation.

(a) *How is a particular measurement to be specified?*

The purpose of the definition is to ensure common and consistent interpretation of the measurement requirements across the whole organization, irrespective of function or location. Specification of the measurement requires identifying the dimension of concern, an appropriate attribute and the key characteristics of that attribute.

For example, for a refrigerator, one "dimension of concern" is the ability of the refrigerator to keep food cold. Attributes that relate to this dimension would be

- the ability of the refrigerator to return to its set temperature after the door is opened for a period
- the actual temperature range experienced for a given setting.

Specific characteristics for these attributes would be

- time in seconds to restore mean temperature
- range in °C for a specific setting.

(b) *How is the measurement to be made?*

This step requires a measurement protocol that specifies how and when the measurement is to occur. It also includes who is responsible for the measurement.

For the refrigerator example, measure: "The ability of the refrigerator to return to its set temperature after the door is opened" using the measure "Time in seconds to restore mean temperature". Then the protocol might be:

1. The test is to be carried out by the Standards Technician and data is to be recorded on Form IX. The electronic door-opening tester is to be used. Ambient temperature is to be set at 25°C.
2. Refrigerators are to be randomly selected from the production line using Sampling Procedure 4.
3. The refrigerator thermostat is to be set at level 5.
4. The refrigerator is to be loaded with Standard Food Load 105.
5. The refrigerator is allowed to reach stable temperature over 48 hours with no door openings.

6. The measurement instrument is to be a calibrated Datamex 302 placed in the centre of the top self. This instrument records temperature to 0.01°C at one-second intervals.
7. The door opening test period is to be thirty seconds repeated at hourly intervals over twenty-four hours.

(c) *How will the data be recorded and stored?*

The protocol will also specify how data are to be recorded and reported.

1. The time to be recorded is the number of seconds for the temperature to return to mean temperature.
2. The data are to be summarized and reported as a mean and standard deviation of the 24 recorded tests on Form IX.
3. All Form IXs are to be retained by the laboratory for two years in date sequence.

Collecting data on opinions

The key issue here is the design of surveys to ensure that "suitable" data are acquired, namely, data that are

- representative of the target group
- sufficient to answer questions with the desired precision
- collected efficiently, without any more effort than necessary.

Censuses (*i.e.* surveying everyone in a target market) are usually impractical in terms of the resources required and, in any event, are usually unnecessary. Generally, a well-designed sample survey will provide sufficiently precise data for the purpose at hand, for much lower cost. (Exceptions would be where the target market comprises a small number of companies, or when all staff in an organization are polled to assess staff satisfaction.)

The issues to be considered in designing a sample survey include

- the purpose of the survey
- selecting the target population and any appropriate stratification

- selecting the type of survey (mail, telephone, personal interview, Internet panel)
- selecting the survey design (simple random sample, stratified *etc.*)
- the desired level of precision required in the answers.

leading to considerations of

- the questions to be asked
- the sample size required
- how the data will be recorded, managed, summarized and analyzed, and
- how the results will be reported.

So the basic concepts to be explored are

- operational definitions
- data collection protocols
- responsibility for data collection
- effectiveness of data collection systems
- surveys.

Questions and considerations

- How are various measures collected throughout the organization?
- How are the instructions for data collection (including when, where and how) documented and standardized?
- The availability of instructions (and how and whether they are used).
- Who has responsibility for acquisition of particular measures and for the quality of data as acquired?
- Availability and use of appropriate and standardized tools, *e.g.* sheets, forms, electronic formats, to assist data collection.
- Are the data fit for purpose by their intended users – timely, representative, trusted, meet their needs *etc.*?

Data analysis and use

While measurement *per se* is an interesting technical topic, its value from a management perspective lies in the ability of the enterprise to transform data into information to inform business decisions, and perhaps to create learning and knowledge.

Data are vital raw materials to feed into the information- and decision-making processes of the organization. Information creation has two main stages:

- data analysis
- presentation of the information resulting from the analysis.

Organizations that have strengths in data analysis and presentation will

- demonstrate high levels of consistency in their use of the various tools and presentation styles
- have a consistent approach to process improvement
- value sound technical problem analysis
- demonstrate appropriate statistical thinking skills and appreciate the impact of variation on their process control
- have appropriate, informative reporting formats for the results of the analysis.

Data analysis techniques include both "soft" approaches based on qualitative data and "hard" approaches using quantitative data. Usually, the people involved in a process can contribute information about a problem and its probable causes, but may need additional data and techniques to resolve the problems. Process improvement methodologies often use both qualitative and quantitative data for problem solving.

Typical approaches to acquiring *qualitative* data include brainstorming, force field analysis, nominal group technique and flowcharting. Typical approaches to acquiring *quantitative* data include running surveys, process capability studies and designed experiments.

Effective presentation of information is a critical input to decision-making. It is imperative to prepare and present information in a format that is easily understood and allows for the appropriate interpretation. Common presentation formats for qualitative data are:

- affinity diagrams
- cause-and-effect diagrams
- radar charts.

Common presentation formats for quantitative data are:

- tables
- dot charts
- run charts
- control charts
- flowcharts
- histograms
- Pareto charts
- scatterplots.

Carrying out appropriate analysis and interpretation requires a certain level of technical skill and knowledge. To maximize the effective conversion of data into information, it is important to develop the relevant skills in staff and managers at all levels of the organization.

So the basic concepts being explored are:

- appropriate data analysis
- group and team methodologies
- statistically based data analysis
- presentation of information
- visual presentation
- appropriate graphics
- appropriate tabular formats
- organizational skills in data analysis and use.

Questions and considerations
- Do staff and managers receive appropriate quantitative information to enable them to manage their work?
- How is information used to assist decision-making?

- Evidence of the use of data analysis in the organization, *e.g.* charting techniques, quality improvement reports, trend charts in leadership team reports, quantification of uncertainty in summary values reported to senior leadership (market share, customer loyalty *etc.*)
- The ability of staff at all levels to interpret the quantitative information that they receive.
- The extent to which data analysis is used to inform decision-making in the organization.
- Relevant training of staff at all levels to give them the skills and knowledge in data analysis that are appropriate to their requirements.
- Use of statistical methods appropriate to the quality of the data and the purpose.
- Appropriate reporting formats. Do people consider that the reports help them do their jobs?
- The extent of understanding about variation and process control. For example, how do people respond to information relating to process performance and capability, to inform fault identification and correction?
- Are the results of the data analysis reaching the right people, in the sense that the recipients have the authority and responsibility to act on the results?

Ongoing review of the measurement system

Organizational performance measurement is a critical component of the management system of any enterprise. Without measurement, there is no good way to make an objective assessment of any aspect of performance.

The overall data requirements of the enterprise will change with time. Accordingly, the performance measurement system needs to be reviewed regularly, in association with other organizational review processes (such as planning).

A review against the Performance Measurement Framework by addressing each criterion of the measurement system serves as an input to the ongoing improvement of the performance measurement approach. The basic concepts being explored are:

- Improvement methodology
- Application of review and improvement processes to the measurement system.

Questions and considerations
- How is the performance measurement approach reviewed:
  - at the strategic level
  - at the tactical level
  - at the operational level?
- What is the evidence of changes being made to the measures employed?
- To what extent are changes in the planning process accompanied by appropriate changes to the measures used?
- To what extent do staff and management feel that the measurement system meets their needs?

12.4 ANALYZING THE DATA FROM THE ASSESSMENT

The assessors now proceed to analyze the data collected from interviews and to assign scores. Again, we suggest using a scoring system similar to those used for assessments against the Baldrige and EFQM frameworks, with some simplification.

In the language of those frameworks, performance measurement would be an *Enabler*. For each of the eight criteria, scoring is done according to two "dimensions": *Approach* and *Deployment*. (The additional dimensions of *Results* and *Improvement* employed by Baldrige and EFQM are not used.)

Factors used to evaluate *Approach* include:

- the appropriateness of the policies, processes and methods used
- the extent to which they are integrated, effective and embody improvement
- alignment with organizational needs.

EXHIBIT 12.5. Criteria used to evaluate levels of effectiveness and maturity of the enterprise performance measurement system. Scores can provide a basis for identifying priorities for improvement and for assessing progress over time.

Score	Approach	Deployment
0	No approach	No deployment
1–2	Beginnings of an approach	Major gaps in deployment
3–4	Some elements of approach developed and documented	Early stages in some areas
5–6	Effective, systematic approach	Well deployed in most areas
7–8	Approach is well integrated with plans, systems and processes	Well deployed with no significant gaps
9–10	Approach is fully developed	Fully deployed in all areas

Note: This is the simplified calibration matrix used by Vogel (2008), page 20.

Factors used to evaluate *Deployment* include:

- the effectiveness of the use of the approach by all appropriate work areas
- the extent to which the approach is part of normal operations and planning.

Scoring for each dimension is done on the scale 0 to 10, as described in Exhibit 12.5.

The assessors first decide on scores individually, compiling them into a so-called "calibration matrix." A prototypical example is shown in shown in Exhibit 12.6. Then they discuss cells in their calibration matrices that show significant difference of opinion. These are resolved and a final matrix produced.

12.5 PREPARING THE REPORT

Experience with reporting the results of Performance Measurement Framework assessments has demonstrated that a report structured as

EXHIBIT 12.6. Example of summary scores by an individual assessor, assembled into a calibration matrix, for an engineering plant. Once assessed individually, assessors meet, discuss significant differences, and agree on a common set of scores.

| Criterion | Scores | | Overall comments |
	A	D	
Strategic measurement	0	0	No stakeholder survey data available, so no measures
Tactical measurement	4	3	Limited to financial, regulatory and basic marketing/staff turnover data
Operational measurement	6	5	Data collection and analysis in place as part of QC of production processes
Role Alignment	6	3	At operational level, technical people aware of their key Accountabilities
Scope of data	4	3	Good operational data where mission-critical, otherwise poor or non-existent
Data collection processes	4	4	Good operational data where mission-critical, otherwise poor or non-existent
Data analysis and use	6	6	Good at operational level where mission-critical, otherwise poor or non-existent. At strategic level, managing by the bottom line
Review of mst. system	2	2	This is the first review of the current use of data and information to inform decision-making
Total	32/80	26/80	

shown in Exhibit 12.7 has worked well, when presenting the feedback workshop. The scores from the calibration matrix provide a quantitative basis for selecting the principal recommendations.

In particular, feeding back the findings in the concise and actionable format shown in Exhibit 11.2 has been particularly effective.

EXHIBIT 12.7. Recommended structure of report to planning workshop, when presenting the results of the assessment of the enterprise's performance measurement system against the Performance Measurement Framework.

Section	Content
1	Cover page: Performance Measurement Diagnostic Assessment
2	Purpose: • Review current performance against the Performance Measurement Framework (PMF) • Identify strengths and opportunities for improvement
3	What was our process? • Interviewed members of XXX leadership and selected members of staff • Examined relevant documents and reports • We appreciated the friendliness and cooperation of all staff
4	Strengths of XXX: • (List of what they are doing well)
5	Approach to issues identified: For each issue identified, we: • detail our perception of the *issue* • present *evidence* we saw of the issue • provide some *recommendations* for addressing the issue • identify the potential *benefits* to XXX from the recommendations
6	Overall calibration matrix: • Numerical results in table • Graphical presentation
7	List of issues: • One issue per page, structured as in Exhibit 10.2 (Statement of issue, Evidence, Recommendation, Likely Benefits)

12.6 CONDUCTING THE FEEDBACK WORKSHOP

The standard technique used in reporting the results of a stakeholder survey works well here. Rather than presenting the results (in this case, the calibration matrix) immediately, it is preferable to run a small process which involves

1. briefing the senior officer about the key findings before the workshop
2. asking the workshop participants to do their own scoring (which could be requested as preparation in advance of the workshop)
3. identifying any areas where there are quite differing scores between the participants, and resolving these disagreements
4. presenting the actual results.

Otherwise, the workshop should be straightforward, given the structure of the report.

NOTES

1 Much of this material was developed by a team in CSIRO who were evaluating the Organisational Performance Measurement (OPM®) on which the Performance Measurement Framework is based. OPM was trialed extensively with SMEs. The team comprised: Mary Barnes, Annette Chennell, Lyn Coulton, Teresa Dickinson, Stan Dransfield, John Field, Nicholas Fisher, Ian Saunders and Doug Shaw.
2 And, of course, Price's Dictum is relevant here (*cf.* Section 2.1).

13 Practical aspects of managing Stakeholder Value

O wad some Power the giftie gie us
To see oursels as ithers see us!

Robert Burns[1]

13.1 PREAMBLE: AN ONGOING DIALOG WITH THE STAKEHOLDER

Relationships are sustained if the partners to the relationship remain in contact, whether by telephone, letter or email, or personal meetings. And your relationships with your stakeholders are no different. You need some form of ongoing dialog with each of the stakeholder groups. The frequency and nature of the dialog may vary, but it has to take place.

The generic process for managing Stakeholder Value provides an ideal vehicle for a constructive dialog. Indeed, a communications plan is an essential concomitant of a properly implemented Value management process, and we'll discuss this explicitly in Section 13.6 below. The most compelling example of such a dialog is a People Value process (although the same applies to all the other stakeholder groups), so it's helpful to look at the steps in the process (Exhibits 13.1 and 13.2) to see the dialog developing (Exhibit 13.3).

Experience with this process confirms strongly that, even in the most hostile of environments (*e.g.* a university)

- there is a large initial and beneficial impact of involving people in the design of the instrument, they enjoy the Focus Groups[2] and also tell other people what they've been doing and why; and
- people will continue to participate in follow-up surveys provided that management responds to the results promptly and sensibly.

which is hardly surprising in retrospect, but it does require verification.

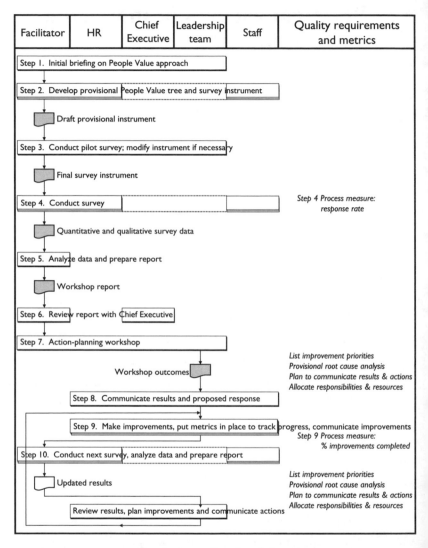

EXHIBIT 13.1. Deployment flowchart[3] describing a way to implement a typical People Value process. This is the top-level chart. The drop shadows indicate a lower-level processes: *e.g.* the sub-process for Step 2 is documented in Exhibit 13.2. The right-most column identifies quality requirements and process metrics.

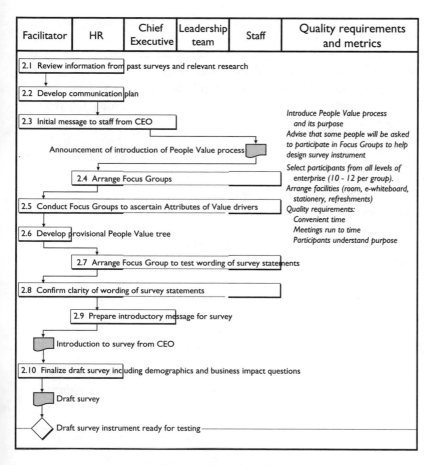

Facilitator	HR	Chief Executive	Leadership team	Staff	Quality requirements and metrics

2.1 Review information from past surveys and relevant research

2.2 Develop communication plan

2.3 Initial message to staff from CEO

Announcement of introduction of People Value process

2.4 Arrange Focus Groups

2.5 Conduct Focus Groups to ascertain Attributes of Value drivers

2.6 Develop provisional People Value tree

2.7 Arrange Focus Group to test wording of survey statements

2.8 Confirm clarity of wording of survey statements

2.9 Prepare introductory message for survey

Introduction to survey from CEO

2.10 Finalize draft survey including demographics and business impact questions

Draft survey

Draft survey instrument ready for testing

Introduce People Value process and its purpose
Advise that some people will be asked to participate in Focus Groups to help design survey instrument
Select participants from all levels of enterprise (10 - 12 per group).
Arrange facilities (room, e-whiteboard, stationery, refreshments)
Quality requirements:
Convenient time
Meetings run to time
Participants understand purpose

EXHIBIT 13.2. Deployment flowchart for Step 2 of the chart in Exhibit 13.1, relating to developing the draft survey instrument.

The rest of this chapter looks at specific practical issues. A lot of implementation issues are covered thoroughly in the book by Kordupleski (2003).

13.2 TYPES OF SURVEY

The four principal ways of carrying out surveys are:

- face-to-face interviews
- telephone interviews
- mail-out surveys
- web-based surveys (possibly using Internet panels).

EXHIBIT 13.3. How a People Value management process facilitates dialog between the leadership and the people.

Step 2.3: CEO announcement	Initial communication from leadership to people	
Step 2.5: Focus Groups		People tell you what's important to them about all aspects of their job
Step 2.8: additional Focus Group	You confirm what you've been told	
Step 4: survey	You ask them how they rate you ...	... and they tell you
Step 8: communicate improvements	You tell them what you've done in response to their feedback	
Step 9: re-survey	You ask them what you need to fix next ...	... and they tell you.
... and so the conversation continues ...		

How does one choose between them, in conducting a Value survey?

There are various criteria one can use to make this decision, the relevant ones depending on the type of stakeholder being surveyed. For example, a Community Value survey would call for consideration of issues of

a. Coverage
b. Precision (quality of responses)
c. Cost
d. Quality of sampling process
e. Speed of response
f. Assurance of anonymity.

Exhibit 13.4 provides a comparison in summary form of the four Community Value survey methods based on these criteria.

EXHIBIT 13.4. Comparison of the relative merits of four different approaches to conducting a Community Value survey.

Criterion	Method			
	Face-to-face interview	Telephone	Mail	Internet panels
Coverage	Potentially, total	Biased	Biased	Biased
Precision	High	Low	Medium	Medium/High
Cost	Very high	High	Medium	Low
Quality of sampling process	High	Low	Low/Medium	Medium/High
Speed of response	Low	Medium	Low	High
Assurance of anonymity	Low	Low	Medium/High	Medium/High

Source: From Fisher *et al.* (2010).

Face-to-face interviews

These are mainly applicable when there are few people to be interviewed. So it would be used for

- Key Account Value management
- developing an individual People Value tree for a key staff member
- developing Partnership Value trees.

Telephone interviews

With the increased amount of tele-marketing that is occurring (and attendant increasing resistance to cooperation by recipients of "cold" marketing calls), the method is steadily losing ground to web-based methods, which have a number of advantages. In particular

- A web-based survey instrument can make more information available to the respondent in relation to each request, should the respondent choose to see it, allowing for more refinement in the query being presented and so less scope for misunderstanding by the respondent.

- There are no transcription issues, eliminating another source of error. The data are captured directly in electronic form.
- It is far easier to provide anonymity of response, allowing respondents to be rather more candid, which can be especially important in People Value surveys.

Consequently, the main value of a telephone interview is as a surrogate for a face-to-face interview.

Mail surveys

Nothing to add to the table.

Web-based surveys

These will be discussed more fully below (Section 13.3). However, in the particular context of Community Value surveys, the topic of Internet panels merits some elaboration.

Internet panels have three main virtues: the speed of the response; the relatively low cost of response; and the fact that this method is completely anonymous for survey panelists, so therefore will generally produce more candid responses.

People are recruited to Internet panels using a variety of methods. Typically, the Internet panel provider has a number of different sites, each with a number of different reward mechanisms to appeal to the varying demographics. People are recruited from these sources according to a range of demographic variables, with a view to building a panel representative of the general population. The process involves prospective members completing a set of profiling questions and a lifestyle survey when first registering. The process is also "double opt in," so the user must confirm his or her status and details before becoming a member.

Of particular interest for Community Value surveys are so-called "ethical" Internet panels. The term "ethical" refers to a number of characteristics of the way the Internet panel is formed, including:

- people are approached and invited to participate, they are not able to apply (*e.g.* by responding to an advertisement for panelists on an Internet dating site)
- there is no guarantee of any reward for panelists, whose motivation is generally an ethical one based on a wish to help society
- panels are refreshed reasonably frequently, and
- there has to be some altruistic purpose for the survey.

For a given survey, email invitations are sent to panelists according to how suitably matched their demographic profile is with the requirements of the survey. This aspect of the process also has protection built in to guard against multiple responses by the same individual.

13.3   DEVELOPING AN INTERNET-BASED SURVEY INSTRUMENT

Many of the practical aspects of implementing Value survey processes are already well documented,[4] so the focus here will be on some recent developments, particularly in relation to creating Internet-based survey instruments.

Making the requests precise

With telephone or paper-based surveys, there is limited scope to make it clear to respondents exactly what information is being requested from them.

In a telephone survey, the caller may or may not have much information at hand to clarify survey statements that are unclear to the respondent. Limited elaboration may be possible; however, once it gets beyond a few clarifications, the flow of the interview is lost, the length of the interview expands, and the patience of the respondent wears thin.

With paper surveys, there is also a limit to the amount of supporting information that can be supplied without producing a very long or very cluttered instrument.

One significant advantage of a web survey instrument in this regard is that information can be concealed until it is required. As an illustration, consider the process of developing a People Value survey instrument. When people are asked about the characteristics of their ideal job, they produce a large number of possible characteristics. These need to be crystallized into a small number – at most six to eight Attributes – without losing the rich variety of ways in which people describe what they want. With a web instrument, this is simple, provided six to eight suitable summaries can be found. Then people are asked to rate the summary Attribute. In case their meaning is not completely clear, the various characteristics feeding into this summary can be made available in bullet-point form in a small pop-up window.

For example, under Work Itself in a People Value survey (see Exhibit 5.3), the survey statement might request that, on a scale of 1 to 10, where 1 = Poor and 10 = Excellent, people rate your enterprise on: "Providing you with stimulating work." What does this mean? The optional extra information might list

- Variety/new experiences
- Opportunity to be creative/use my imagination
- Intellectually challenging
- Uses all my skills/able to work to my full potential
- Enjoyable/fun
- Feeling of achievement/able to achieve completion/produce tangible products/see results/contribute
- Creating productivity/process improvement
- Tailored to my capabilities
- Provides me with the opportunity to teach/share my knowledge

which are all characteristics that emerged from the Focus Groups. Not all of these need apply to you; however, some of them certainly should.

Similarly, under *Work Environment*, the statement: "Providing you with the appropriate support services to your job," the optional extra information might list

- Services are timely and fit-for-purpose
- Efficient and effective information and knowledge management
- IT and communications support
- Human Resources, Engineering, OHS, Quality, Environment, Legal, Marketing, Inventory Control, management of stakeholders *etc.*
- Administrative support
- Up-to-date subcontractor database.

Scale of responses

Many traditional surveys use a 5-point or 7-point scale for responses. The small number of options becomes even smaller when one finds, in practice, that people are loath to use the two extreme values, leading to poor discriminatory power in the responses. There is now strong evidence that a 10-point scale provides two powerful benefits:

- It provides respondents with the ability to make reasonably fine distinctions.[5]
- The scale is sufficiently fine that the responses can be regarded as continuous, and statistical methods appropriate to continuous data can be applied.[6]

Also, it helps to include DK (*Don't Know*) and NA (*Not Applicable*) to the range of possible responses to Attributes (but not for drivers) to avoid forcing a response where none may be possible.

The introductory statement

The survey introduction by the CEO needs to include information about how the results will be used; it may also be appropriate to advise respondents how the results and response will be communicated. If the identity of respondents is to remain anonymous, assurance of this needs to be provided here or immediately afterwards.

Demographic factors

It is important to collect as much demographic information as is possible. This leads to greater capability of statistical models to explain what's happening in the data. However, two issues arise that conflict with this:

1. If you have guaranteed anonymity of response, this will limit the total combination of factors and levels of each factor. So, if you intend to use:
   - Gender (Female/Male)
   - Age (below 25, 25 to 50, above 50)
   - Length of time in current position (up to 2 years, 2 to 5, 5 to 10 years, over 10 years)
   - Location of office (city/regional center/rural)
   - Highest level of education received (High School/University/ Graduate studies)

   in a People Value survey, you have a total of $2 \times 3 \times 4 \times 3 \times 3 = 216$ possible combinations, which might well suffice to identify some respondents uniquely.
2. Ensuring that there are sufficient data available for each demographic combination for which a statistical model is supposed to be fitted. In our experience, at least thirty responses (and preferably fifty) are needed for each factor combination to produce results on which one can place any reliance. With fewer data, the results are too imprecise to be actionable.

Samples rather than censuses

This is particularly important with People Value surveys. Bear in mind what's being sought from the survey data: timely and actionable information to help you identify those priorities for improvement likely to have the biggest impact on the business. "Timely" means that you need the information at least twice, if not three times a year. (How would you manage if you received your financial reports annually? All you'd be able to do would be to react to disasters that had happened because you weren't getting information sufficiently frequently. The same happens with People or Customers.) However, that *doesn't* mean you have to survey everyone twice or three times a year.

You just need a sufficient number of *carefully selected* respondents to build reliable statistical models – in other words, at least thirty for each combination of demographic factors.

What does "carefully selected" mean? It means that people have been selected at random, but in such a way as to ensure that there are sufficient numbers for each demographic factor to ensure a balanced data set. A well-known statistical tool known as *stratified sampling* provides this assurance, and is simple to implement.

13.4 ANALYZING THE DATA AND PREPARING A REPORT

A very simple approach to fitting the basic regression models seems to suffice:

1. Fit a least squares model.
2. Set negative coefficients to zero.
3. Use coefficients as Impact weights, normalized to add to the value of R^2.

The usual adjustments for multi-collinearity can be made. (However, any Attributes eliminated in this way should be retained in the model and the Value tree; see Kordupleski (2003), page 193.) Another awkward issue can arise when respondents to a Community Value survey become confused about the meaning of high or low ratings. For example, in Exhibit 8.2, respondents may mistakenly assign a rating of 9 to the possibility that a virus may jump species, supposedly meaning that they are reasonably unconcerned about this, whereas they are very concerned, and so should have assigned a rating of 2. This can become evident when one reads associated comments. Fisher and Lee (2011) have developed a device for coping with this situation.

There are a few points to look for when your data are analyzed and a report prepared:

- Make sure that useless responses have been removed. When a respondent has given the same numerical response to every single request (*e.g.* assigned a score of 10 to every request), these are best eliminated. Firstly, no thought has gone into the response. Secondly, and more importantly, the more extreme the response, the greater the potential to distort the analysis. Definitely screen out answers that are all 1s or all 10s, and probably remove the less extreme mono-responses as well.

- When reporting the results, ensure that:
  - each mean value (typically reported to one decimal place) is accompanied by an estimate of its precision, either a standard error or a 95 percent confidence interval, and an explanation of how this precision is to be interpreted
  - figures and tables have fully self-explanatory captions
  - graphs and tables are used appropriately. The purpose of a table is to show numerical information as precisely as is justified. The purpose of a graph is to display a pattern. And the choice of graphs matters. Poor graphs may distort the pattern to the point of being quite misleading. Well-constructed graphs can be quite striking in their impact[7]
  - tabular or graphical comparisons (e.g. boxplots or point-and-interval displays) provide some information about which group or groups differ from which others in a statistically meaningful way.

13.5 THE PLANNING WORKSHOP

Planning workshops are slightly different for Partner surveys and for Board evaluations by the executive leadership than for Customer, People and Community surveys, so we'll discuss those situations separately. (The process for Board assessment of the enterprise was essentially covered in Section 8.4.)

Planning workshops for Customer, People and Community surveys

As we noted earlier, Ray Kordupleski has devoted a whole chapter of his book[8] to this vital aspect of managing Customer Value, from which there is much to be learned, so we offer just a brief summary here.

EXHIBIT 13.5. Outline of planning workshop for reporting the results of a Value Management survey.

Create understanding	1. Workshop purpose, Objectives, Outcomes • Outlined by team leader 2. Overview of Value Management concepts and tools, positioned in broader performance measurement context • Presented by subject matter expert
Gain acceptance	3. Predict research findings • Individual and small group learning exercise 4. Present research findings • Presentation and group discussion
Plan actions	5. Select priorities • Individual and small group learning exercise/ group discussion 6. Set targets and develop provisional action plans • Small group exercise 7. Present plans • Small groups present to large group and team leader 8. Plan how to communicate the results and outcomes to relevant groups • Group discussion

Exhibit 13.5 is a modified version of a helpful diagram for the overall workshop process appearing on page 206 of Kordupleski's Chapter 11. We comment briefly on each step, referring the reader to Kordupleski's book for the operational details.

An important initial step is not shown in the exhibit, but we insert it here.

0. Brief the senior officer about the key results, particularly anything unusual.

   The basic principle is: *No surprises*. If there is an issue that will require careful management, the officer needs to be given the opportunity to develop a strategy in advance.

1. Workshop purpose, Objectives, Outcomes

   It is critical that the workshop be opened by a senior officer of the enterprise, someone with the authority to ensure that actions arising from the workshop will, indeed, be carried out.

2. Overview of Value Management concepts and tools, positioned in broader performance measurement context:

   - If the workshop relates to managing Customer Value, then the key elements of Chapter 4 can be presented, in the context of Customers being one of 5 main stakeholder groups (Section 3.4).

   - For a workshop relating to the results of a People or Community Value survey, it helps to outline the broad performance measurement context initially (Section 3.4), provide a brief version of managing Customer Value as the core approach, and then, by analogy, explain the modifications for this particular context.

3. Predict research findings

   The workshop participants develop their best guess at how the market (Customer/People/Community) view them – the relative importance of the top-level drivers in determining stakeholder perceptions, and the mean ratings the stakeholder group has assigned. This gets the participants thinking, or at least attempting to think, from the stakeholder perspective. Participants should do initial assessments individually, then the facilitator works with them to develop a group assessment, probing reasons for disparate allocations of Impact weights, or widely differing ratings.

   Another, almost completely obvious, reason for this step is so that the people have explicitly attempted to "read the market's mind." The reaction "Just as I thought" when the actual results are presented is then largely avoided (except, of course, for those who guessed the results exactly).

4. Present research findings

   Participants are now confronted with reality, providing the
   basis for an interesting and productive discussion. *Note that
   the focus is on the quantitative results.* There will, of course, be a
   wealth of comments associated with reasons for assigning
   ratings to Value and its drivers. Indeed, it may be helpful to
   crystallize a few messages from these comments to illuminate
   particular ratings. However, it is best *not* to present the qualitative
   data, at least early on. Possibly, this report can be made available for
   Step 6, with comments arranged by business unit, and then sorted
   on ratings.

   - The numbers help identify where to focus attention.
   - The comments *may* provide insight into root causes, once the
     areas for improvement have been identified.

5. Select priorities

   This is where the basic Value analysis tools come into play: the
   Value Map, profiles of top-level results, Loyalty curves. Where do
   you need to be in twelve months' time? Where are you performing
   below par? Where do you want to be superior (*e.g.* on Quality and
   Image for a Customer Value survey) and where are you prepared to
   be at par (*e.g.* Price)? For Quality, look at profiles such as Exhibits
   5.9 and 5.10, to identify where to focus attention; similarly for
   Image and Price.

6. Set targets and develop provisional action plans

   This can be done in small groups, *e.g.* for a Customer Value survey,
   one group might look at Quality, another at Price, and another at
   Image. What can be done to improve the ratings in each selected
   area?

   - What might be causing the problems?
   - Are there underlying process or systemic issues?
   - Is there some insight to be gleaned from the qualitative data?
   - What sort of improvement in Attribute ratings might be feasible?

7. Present plans

The individual plans are now discussed, and provisional decisions made about:

- appropriate cross-functional teams to address the problems
- who's leading each team, resourcing the team, and when it should report
- the next round of surveying (unless surveying continuously, in which case, the next round of reporting).

8. Plan how to communicate the results and plans to relevant groups

People have taken the trouble to complete the survey. Now they are expecting action. So some of the issues here are:

- How will the results be communicated throughout your enterprise?
- Workshops similar to this one?
- Which senior officers will attend them or, indeed, run them?
- For a Customer Value or Community Value survey, how will the results be communicated to the stakeholder group?

Planning workshops for Partnership Value surveys

Workshops relating to a Supplier Value survey would not be different from what we've already discussed. However, modifications are needed for planning workshops associated with Alliances or Co-ventures. In such cases, the participants in the workshop have rated each other. So some steps from 3 onwards in Exhibit 13.5 need modification in fairly obvious ways, e.g.:

3*.   Predict research findings:
      Small group work: Participants from each Partner organization need to guess how they were assessed by the other Partner(s).

5*.   Select priorities:
      This now becomes a joint exercise with all sides present.

Steps 6–8 may now be done by the whole group, or it may make sense to do some small group work, depending on the nature of the issues to be addressed (*e.g.* internal to a particular Partner) or the total number of participants (*e.g.* with fewer than seven or eight people, it may not be worth splitting up).

Planning workshops for Board Assessment surveys

In this situation, the executive leadership has evaluated the Board (see Section 8.5). Again, some steps from 3 onwards in Exhibit 13.5 need modification in fairly obvious ways, *e.g.*:

3*.   Predict research findings:
      The Board has to guess how the executive group has rated them.
      This can be done in advance of the workshop, to save time.
5*.   Select priorities:
      This now becomes a joint exercise with all sides present.

Steps 6–8 may then be done by the whole group or some work may be done in the two smaller groups, depending on the issues raised.

13.6   THE VALUE SURVEY COMMUNICATIONS PLAN

Here, we'll describe a prototypical communications plan associated with a People Value process. The key point to bear in mind is that the process is facilitating an ongoing dialog between your enterprise and the particular stakeholder group of interest.

Successfully implementing a People Value Management (PVM) process depends critically on communicating each phase of the implementation clearly to the people in the organization.

The goals of the communication plan are to provide everyone in the organization with a clear understanding of:

a. the purpose of the PVM process
b. their role in implementing the process
c. how the results of the surveys will be used and publicized, and
d. what happens after the first survey.

The following summary steps are recommended.

	Purpose	Who	Timing
1.	Announce introduction of process, and address (a) – (d) above.	MD/CEO/GM	At the beginning.
2.	Invite people to participate in Focus Groups to determine drivers of satisfaction.	HR Manager	1–2 weeks before FGs.
3.	Invite people to participate in Focus Groups to test statements in survey instruments.	HR Manager	1–2 weeks before FGs.
4.	Message on survey instrument.	MD/CEO/GM	When survey instrument is being designed.
5.	Invite people to participate in pilot survey.	HR Manager	1 week before email request sent, with username and password.
6.	Invite people to participate in main survey.	HR Manager	1 week before email request sent, with username and password.
7.	Announce survey results and planned executive response.	MD/CEO/GM	
8.	Announce outcomes of planned response, and initialization of ongoing survey process.	MD/CEO/GM	

The details of these steps are set out below.

Step 1: General announcement

From:	Senior officer (CEO/MD/GM)
To:	All staff
Purpose:	Announce introduction of process and address (a) – (c) above
Typical content:	1. The purpose of the PVM process

1. The purpose of the PVM process
   - Help leadership team establish its priorities for improving all aspects of people's working life.
2. Their role in implementation of the process
   - Survey to be carried out by an independent consultant.
   - The survey itself will be relatively short, and people should be able to complete it in 10–12 minutes. It will be carried out electronically, with people logging into a secure site hosted by an independent organization. Respondents will be given special login names and passwords to protect their anonymity.
   - Some people will be asked to participate in Focus Groups that will be used to identify the most important factors determining people's satisfaction with their work and remuneration. This information will form the basis of the survey.
   - Another group of people will be asked to participate in a pilot survey, to make sure that the survey instrument has been designed well.
3. How the results of the surveys will be used and publicized.
   - Results of the survey will be made available to all people, together with the actions that the leadership team will be taking in response to the findings.
4. What happens after the first survey?
   - The process will continue as a rolling survey, with people being asked, perhaps once or twice a year, to log into the web site and complete it. Results and intended responses will be published regularly.

Step 2: Message to participants in Focus Groups to determine attributes of key drivers of satisfaction

From:	Senior officer (CEO/MD/GM) or HR Manager
To:	Focus Group participants
Purpose:	Invite people to participate in a Focus Group
Typical content:	• As you will be aware from [previous announcement] we are introducing a Staff Satisfaction survey process.
	• This will be based on a customized survey instrument that focuses on the key factors affecting your satisfaction with your work and remuneration.
	• You are requested to participate in one of the Focus Groups that will be seeking to identify these factors. This will take about 90 minutes. Lunch/light refreshments will be provided.

Step 3: Message to participants in Focus Groups to test phrasing of statements in survey

From:	Senior officer (CEO/MD/GM) or HR Manager
To:	Focus Group participants
Purpose:	Invite people to participate in a Focus Group
Typical content:	• As you will be aware from [previous announcement] we are introducing a Staff Satisfaction survey process.
	• This will be based on a customized survey instrument that focuses on the key factors affecting your satisfaction with your work and remuneration.
	• You are requested to participate in one of the Focus Groups that will be finalizing the statements in the survey. It will take about 90 minutes. Lunch/light refreshments will be provided.

Step 4: Message at top of survey instrument

From:	Senior officer (CEO/MD/GM)
To:	Respondents
Purpose:	Remind people of purpose of survey, when they log in Introduction – Message from the CEO

Typical
content:

CORPX is seeking to improve your satisfaction with your working life in CORPX, and with the pay and benefits you receive. The purpose of this survey is to ascertain how you currently rate CORPX on a number of factors that are likely to affect your satisfaction with working here. This will serve as a guide to the CEO and the senior leadership in selecting priorities for improving all aspects of people's work.

The survey is quite short, and should take you at most 10–12 minutes to complete, apart from any comments you may wish to make. It has sections relating to:

- the work you do
- your work environment
- the culture of your organization
- the external image of your organization
- your financial package
- your non-financial package
- some overall issues
- some demographic information.

The first six of these fit into a tree structure, called a Value tree.

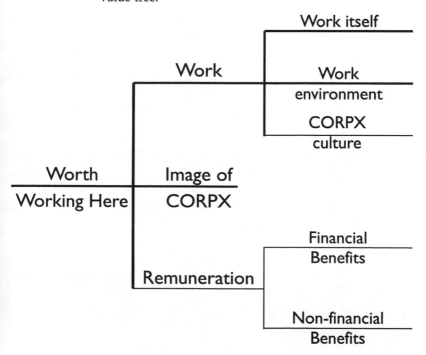

Later in the survey, there will be overall questions relating to the higher-level (summary) factors, Work and Remuneration, and finally, Worth Working Here.

The survey will be conducted by external consultants, with the survey instrument itself being hosted on a remote secure web site. Any identifiers will be stripped from the data file prior to analysis, to ensure your anonymity when the results are reported to management.

The results of the survey, together with the Leadership's planned response, will be made available to all staff members as soon as possible.

[If, for some reason, your session is terminated before you are able to complete the survey, you can log in again. If you log in on the same day, the survey information you have already entered will be available; otherwise, you will need to complete the full survey.]

Step 5: Message to participants in the pilot study to test the survey instrument

From:	Senior officer (CEO/MD/GM) or HR Manager
To:	Participants in Pilot Study
Purpose:	Ask people to participate in the pilot survey
Typical content:	• As you will be aware from [previous announcement] we are introducing a Staff Satisfaction survey process.
	• This will be based on a customized survey instrument that focuses on the key factors affecting your satisfaction with your work and remuneration.
	• You are asked to participate in a pilot study to test that the survey instrument is ready for general use. You will not be asked to respond again, when the main survey is carried out a couple of weeks later.
	• The survey will be carried out during [dates], and it will be done electronically. It should take about 10–12 minutes to complete. You will receive an email message requesting you to log on to a web site, and providing you with a username and password. This is a secure site unconnected with [your organization] and the username and password have been assigned purely to

monitor who has responded. They will not be associated with your response, so your anonymity will be assured.

- The survey results will be made available to all people, together with the intended response by the leadership team.

Step 6: Message to participants in the main survey

From:	Senior officer (CEO/MD/GM) or HR Manager
To:	Participants in main survey
Purpose:	Ask people to participate in the main survey
Typical content:	• As you will be aware from [previous announcement] we are introducing a Staff Satisfaction survey process.
	• This will be based on a customized survey instrument that focuses on the key factors affecting your satisfaction with your work and remuneration.
	• You are asked to participate in the survey, which will be carried out during [dates]. It will be done electronically, and should take about 10–12 minutes to complete. You will receive an email message requesting you to log on to a web site, and providing you with a username and password. This is a secure site unconnected with [your organization] and the username and password have been assigned purely to monitor who has responded. They will not be associated with your response, so your anonymity will be assured.
	• The survey results will be made available to all people, together with the intended response by the leadership team.

Step 7: Covering email message to participants in the pilot survey

From:	External facilitator
To:	Participants in CORPX pilot Staff Satisfaction survey
Subject:	CORPX pilot Staff Satisfaction survey
Typical content:	Further to the message sent to you a few weeks ago, CORPX are adopting a process for monitoring Staff Satisfaction on an ongoing basis, in order to identify and

respond to the most important factors affecting your overall satisfaction with working at CORPX.

A provisional survey is now ready for testing. You are one of the CORPX employees who has been selected at random to test the survey. It should only take about 10–12 minutes to complete, and your response will be kept anonymous. Also, you will not be re-contacted when the rest of the staff are surveyed.

Please log onto www.xxx.yyy.zzz as soon as convenient to complete the survey. It contains more information about its purpose, and how the results will be used.

Thank you for your cooperation.

Step 8: Covering email message to participants in the main survey

From:	External facilitator
To:	Participants in CORPX pilot Staff Satisfaction survey
Subject:	CORPX pilot Staff Satisfaction survey
Typical content:	Further to the message sent to you a few weeks ago, CORPX are adopting a process for monitoring Staff Satisfaction on an ongoing basis, in order to identify and respond to the most important factors affecting your overall satisfaction with working at CORPX.

You are now being requested to respond to the survey. It should only take about 10–12 minutes to complete, and your response will be kept anonymous.

Please log onto www.xxx.yyy.zzz as soon as convenient to complete the survey. It contains more information about its purpose, and how the results will be used.

Thank you for your cooperation.

13.7   RUNNING A CONTINUOUS SURVEY

Such surveys were illustrated in the context of People Value (Section 6.5) and Community Value (Section 8.5). Continuously acquired survey data can provide vital and timely information that enables the enterprise to confirm that a past action has been effective or, perhaps more importantly, to recognize that action is required promptly to capitalize on an opportunity or avoid an impending disaster.

Continuous surveys are particularly well-suited to fast-moving markets – Customer, People or Community. The information obtained is far richer than from static surveys run, perhaps, every six months. They retain all the benefits of a static survey:

- focusing on the most important factors driving overall satisfaction;
- producing actionable reports;
- facilitating identification of most important improvement priorities.

while offering timely warnings of:

- important shifts in perception of the performance of your enterprise; and
- important shifts in the relative importance of Attributes and drivers, in determining overall Stakeholder Value.

The key issue in implementing such surveys is to ensure that, over each period of (say) thirteen weeks, the sample of respondents is balanced in terms of the various demographic factors of interest. Again, this is a straightforward application of stratified random sampling. Analysis of the resulting data requires suitable statistical algorithms to be implemented.[9]

NOTES

1 Robert Burns, "To a Louse. On Seeing one on a Lady's bonnet at Church." The poem begins

> Ha! whare ye gaun, ye crawlin ferlie!
> Your impudence protects you sairlie
> I canna say but ye strunt rarely
> Owre gauze and lace
> Tho' faith, I fear, ye dine but sparely
> On sic a place

Ye ugly, creepin, blastit wonner
Detested, shunn'd, by saunt an' sinner
How daur ye set your fit upon her
Sae fine a Lady!
Gae somewhere else and seek your dinner
On some poor body

and so on, and concludes with

O wad some Power the giftie gie us
To see oursels as ithers see us!
It wad frae mony a blunder free us,
An' foolish notion:
What airs in dress and gait would leave us,
And even devotion!

which has been translated as (http://www.robertburns.plus.com/louse.htm)

Oh, that God would give us the very smallest of gifts
To be able to see ourselves as others see us
It would save us from many mistakes
and foolish thoughts
We would change the way we look and gesture
and to how and what we apply our time and attention.

2 When running a Focus Group, it sometimes helps to say at the outset that the purpose is to identify the most important Attributes of an ideal relationship — *e.g.* (for a People Value survey) in the best of all possible worlds, what are all the characteristics of your Work, the Image of the enterprise, and how you're remunerated?

3 A flowchart is a diagrammatic representation of the steps of a process as it is now, or as it might be designed. A *deployment* flowchart adds an extra dimension of information that shows who carries out the steps identified in the process; that is, it shows how people or groups involved in the process are deployed against the various tasks to be carried out. Omitting this aspect means running the risk of omitting the place where most problems occur: in

the interaction between the people and the process. It is, in Myron Tribus'
view, the single most important tool in management.

It has other important properties:

1. A vertical line descending into a meeting box shows who called the
   meeting.
2. *Every horizontal line indicates a customer–supplier relationship* (where
   both customer and supplier can be internal to the organization), *and
   hence the opportunity to measure conformance with the customer's
   needs.*
3. The column at the right hand side contains information like:
   - opportunities to make measurements (*e.g.* internal or external
     customer requirements as noted in (2); the number of times around a
     loop in the flowchart; or cycle time for a process or sub–process);
   - issues to consider in association with a process step;
   - reference to relevant document (*e.g.* a standardized procedure, or the
     location of a sub–process relating to a replicated shape – *cf.* (2)).

When constructing a flowchart, it is best to keep the number of symbols on
a particular chart to about 12–15. A replicated shape indicates that there is a
sub-process associated with this process step, which is documented
elsewhere.

4 Kordupleski (2003).
5 *Ibid.*
6 Clark *et al.* (1997).
7 See Cleveland and Fisher (1998) and references therein for a comparative
   discussion, with examples.
8 Kordupleski (2003), Chapter 11.
9 See *e.g.* Fisher *et al.* (2005).

14 Performance measurement for Small and Medium Enterprises

Small and Medium Enterprises (SMEs) need performance measurement systems too! Indeed, the Performance Measurement Framework described in Chapter 2 was developed initially in the context of seeking to assist SMEs with a widespread weakness in the way they conducted business. And this weakness continues: for example, Antonio Lerro comments[1]

> Despite companies increasingly recognising the relevance of a stakeholder value-based approach to their business, often they still do not clearly identify their key stakeholders and the related wants and needs, and consequently their value propositions as well as the value creation mechanisms and the impact of the value creation dynamics on the different stakeholders. This is particularly the case of the small and medium enterprises (SMEs) which generally manage implicitly their strategic value positioning. In addition, it is important to stress that although value-based approaches are recognised as being fundamental to organizational success, the tools for identifying, assessing and measuring organizational value for key stakeholders and the impact on the economic and social systems are still inadequate.

For an SME, adopting a performance measurement system is rather simpler than for a larger enterprise.

1. The starting point is the stakeholder analysis described in Section 11.3: who are the principal parties (sub-groups) in each stakeholder group, and what are their main issues (*e.g.* Exhibit 11.2)?
2. Given your current business issues, where do you need to focus attention first – Customers? People? Partners? Community? – and which sub-groups of these?

3. For an SME, the number of customers, or the number of people employed, may be too small to warrant full surveys. However, Focus Groups can certainly be conducted to ascertain the key Attributes of the Value drivers, and then the same (and possibly additional) Focus Groups used to gather some basic data on the relative importance of the various Value drivers, and of how your enterprise is rated, relative to your competitors. That should provide a reasonable basis for setting priorities to improve your business.

NOTE

1 Lerro (2011).

Appendix: Don't be fooled by statistics

The only statistics I trust are those I made up myself.

W. S. Churchill

There is no data that can be displayed in a pie chart, that cannot be displayed BETTER in some other type of chart.

John W. Tukey

Numerical quantities focus on expected values, graphical summaries on unexpected values.

John W. Tukey

I never touch statistics. I just deal with the facts.

F. J. Vine[1]

Lucky Fred (Vine)! Unfortunately, the rest of us have to deal with the real world, which is pervaded by uncertainty. It behoves anyone being presented with quantitative information in the form of individual numbers, tables and graphs to gain an understanding of what all this stuff means. After all, if it's being presented to you, you may well be accountable for what it all implies. So, to help you elicit this information, here are some basic questions to ask.

1. How reliable is this number?/What sort of error do you associate with this number?
2. How do you know it has changed significantly from last month's (last quarter's) number?
3. Where is the trend chart for these numbers?
4. Is that apparent increase/decrease/cyclic effect in this trend chart really meaningful?
5. What is the justification for using so many significant digits/ decimal points?

6. How representative was the sample used to calculate these numbers? How was the sample collected? What biases might be present? How do you know you collected sufficient data to produce a reliable estimate? What demographic factors do you think might affect this number?

7. Why are you presenting a pie chart instead of a dot chart?[2]

8. Why are you presenting a divided bar chart instead of some dot charts?

9. If we're supposed to be seeing a pattern in the data, why aren't we looking at graphs instead of tables?

10. How do you predict these numbers will change in the future, and what is the uncertainty in your forecasts?

11. Why is this a realistic target? How do you know the system is capable of achieving it?

NOTES

1 Vine (1968).

2 For a simple guide to basic graphs see Cleveland and Fisher (1998).

References

Atkinson, Anthony A., John H. Waterhouse and Robert B. Wells (1997), "A Stakeholder Approach to Strategic Performance measurement," *Sloan Management Review*, Spring 1997 **38** (3), 25–37.

Baggini, Julian (2011), "How Steve Jobs changed capitalism," available at www.guardian.co.uk/technology/2011/oct/06/steve-jobs-changed-capitalism.

Ballow, John, Robert J. Thomas and Göran Roos (2004), "Future value: the $7 trillion challenge," *Journal of Applied Corporate Finance* **16** (1), 71–6

Bertini, Marco and John T. Gourville (2012), "Pricing to create shared value," *Harvard Business Review* **90** (6) (June), 96–104.

Byrne, John A. (1998), "How Al Dunlap self-destructed: The inside story of what drove Sunbeam's board to act," *Business Week*, July 6, 1998, available at www.businessweek.com/1998/27/b3585090.htm.

Chambers, R. J. (1986), *Financial Management*, fourth edition. North Ryde, NSW: Law Book Company.

Chatterji, Aaron and David Levine (2006), "Breaking down the Wall of Codes: Evaluating non-financial performance measurement," *California Management Review* **48** (2), 29–51.

Clark, Linda A., William S. Cleveland, Lorraine Denby and Chuanhai Liu (1997), "Modeling Customer Survey Data," pages 3–57 in C. Gatsonis, R. E. Kass, B. Carlin, A. Carriquiry, A. Gelman, I. Verdinelli, and M. West (1999), editors, *Case Studies in Bayesian Statistics*, Volume IV (Lecture Notes in Statistics / 140), New York: Springer.

Cleveland, W. S. and N. I. Fisher (1998), "Good graphs for better business," *The Quality Magazine* **7** (4), 64–8.

Cribb, Julian and Sari Tjempaka (2009), *Open Science*, Melbourne: CSIRO Publishing.

Davenport, Thomas H. and Jeanne G. Harris (2007), *Competing on Analytics: The New Science of Winning*, Boston, Mass.: Harvard Business School Press.

Davenport, Thomas H., Jeanne G. Harris and Robert Morison (2010), *Analytics at Work: Smarter Decisions, Better Results*, Boston, Mass.: Harvard Business School Press.

Deming, W. Edwards (1994), *The New Economics for Industry, Government Education*, second edition, Cambridge, Mass.: Massachusetts Institute of Technology Center for Advanced Engineering Study.

Dransfield, S. B., N. I. Fisher and N. J. Vogel (1999), "Using statistics and statistical thinking to improve organizational performance: With discussion and authors' reply," *International Statistical Review* **67**, 99–150.

Dull, Stephen F., Wilhelm A. Mohn and Thomas Norén (1995), "Partners," *The McKinsey Quarterly*, 1995 (4), 63–72.

Eccles, Robert G. (1991), "The Performance Measurement Manifesto," *Harvard Business Review* **69** (1), January–February, 131–7.

Eccles, Robert G. (2012), "The future of integrated sustainability reporting," created November, 26 2012, available at www.greenbiz.com/print/49485.

Evenson, R. E., and L. E. Westphal (1995), "Technological Change and Technological Strategy," in J. Behrman and T. N. Srinivasan, editors, *Handbook of Development Economics*, **3** (1), 1995, Amsterdam: North-Holland.

Fisher, N.I. (2009), "Homer Sarasohn and American involvement in the evolution of Quality Management in Japan, 1945–1950," *International Statistical Review* **77**, 276–99.

Fisher, N. I., J. H. J. Cribb and A. J. Peacock (2008), "Reading the public mind: a novel approach to improving the adoption of new science and technology," *Australian Journal of Experimental Agriculture* **47**, 1–10.

Fisher, N. I. and A. J. Lee (2011), "Getting the 'correct' answer from incorrect survey responses: a simple application of the EM algorithm," *Austral. and New Zealand J. Statist.* **53**, 353–64.

Fisher, N.I., A. J. Lee and J. H. J. Cribb (2012), "A scientific approach to monitoring public perceptions of scientific issues," *International Journal of Science Education Part B*, 1–27, iFirst Article.

Fisher, N. I., A. J. Lee, J. H. J. Cribb and G. D. Haynes (2010), "Public perceptions of foxes and fox eradication in Tasmania," *Australian Zoologist*, **35** (3), 576–89.

Fisher, N. I., A. J. Lee and R. S. Sparks (2005), "No more static," *Marketing Research*, Spring 2005,14–19.

Fisher, N. I. and V. N. Nair (2008), "Quality Management and Quality Practice: Perspectives on their History and their Future," *Applied Stochastic Models in Business and Industry*, **25**, 1–28.

Fitz-Enz, Jac (1978), "The measurement imperative," *Personnel Journal* **57** (April), 193–5.

Fitz-Enz, Jac (2013), "How to stop wasting your human capital," *CFO*, January 18, 2013, available at www3.cfo.com/article/2013/1/people_jac-fitz-enz-rop-human-capital-management-?currpage=2.

Franco-Santos, Monica, Mike Kennerley, Pietro Micheli, Veronica Martinez, Steve Mason, Bernard Marr, Dina Gray and Andrew Neely (2007), "Towards a definition of a business performance measurement system," *International Journal of Operations and Production Management* **27** (8), 784–801.

Goh, Swee C. (2012), "Making performance measurement systems more effective in public sector organizations," *Measuring Business Excellence* **16** (1), 31–42.

Goldratt, E. M. (1990), *The Haystack Syndrome: Sifting Information Out of the Data Ocean*, Croton-on-Hudson, N.Y.: North River Press, Inc.

Huselid, Mark A., Brian E. Becker and Richard W. Beatty (2005), *The Workforce Scorecard: Managing Human Capital To Execute Strategy*, Cambridge, Mass.: Harvard Business Press Books.

Kaplan, Robert S. and Anette Mikes (2012), "Managing risks: A new framework," *Harvard Business Review* **90** (6) (June), 48–60.

Kaplan, Robert S. and David P. Norton (1992), "The Balanced Scorecard – measures that drive performance," *Harvard Business Review* **70** (1) (January–February), 71–9.

Kaplan, Robert S. and David P. Norton (1996a), "Using the Balanced Scorecard as a Strategic Management System," *Harvard Business Review* **70** (1) (January–February), 75–85.

Kaplan, Robert S. and David P. Norton (1996b), *The Balanced Scorecard: Translating Strategy Into Action*, Boston, Mass.: Harvard Business School Press.

Kaplan, Robert S. and David P. Norton (2006), *Alignment: Using the Balanced Scorecard to Create Corporate Synergies*, Boston, Mass.: Harvard Business School Press.

Kordupleski, R. (2003), *Mastering Customer Value Management*, Cincinnati, Ohio: Pinnaflex Educational Resources, Inc.

Lerro, Antonio (2011), "A stakeholder-based perspective in the value impact assessment of the project 'Valuing intangible assets in Scottish renewable SMEs,'" *Measuring Business Excellence* **15** (3), 3–15.

Lev, Baruch (2001), *Intangibles: Management, Measurement and Reporting*, Washington, DC: Brookings Institution Press.

Lev, Baruch, Suresh Radhakrishnan and Weining Zhang (2009), "Organizational capital," *ABACUS*, **45** (3), 275–98.

Likierman, Andrew (2009), "The five traps of performance measurement," *Harvard Business Review* **87** (October), 96–101.

McGregor, Douglas (1960), *The Human Side of Enterprise*, New York: McGraw-Hill.

Neely, Andy (2007), editor, *Business Performance Measurement*, second edition, Cambridge: Cambridge University Press.

Neely, Andy, Mike Kennerly and Chris Adams (2007), "Performance Measurement Frameworks: a review," pages 143–62 in Neely (2007).

Normann, Richard (2001), *Service Management: Strategy and Leadership in Service Business*, third edition, Chichester: John Wiley and Sons.

Normann, Richard and Rafael Ramirez (1994), *Designing Interactive Strategy: From Value Chain to Value Constellation*, Chichester: John Wiley and Sons.

Otley, David (2007), "Accounting performance measurement: A review of its purposes and practices," pages 11–35 in Neely (2007).

Parmenter, David (2010), *Key Performance Indicators*, second edition. Hoboken, N.J.: John Wiley and Sons.

Porter, Michael E. and Mark R. Kramer (2011), "Creating shared value," *Harvard Business Review* 89 (1) (January–February), 62–77.

Price, Frank (1984), *Right First Time*, Aldershot: Wildwood House.

Reichheld, Frederick F. (2003), "One number you need to grow," *Harvard Business Review* 81 (12) (December), 45–64.

Rucci, Anthony J., Steven P. Kirn and Richard T. Quinn (1998), "The Employee – Customer – Profit Chain at Sears," *Harvard Business Review*, 72 (1) (January–February), 82–97.

Rybka, Zdeněk (2008), *Principles of the Bata Management System*, second edition. Zlín: Faculty of Management and Economics, Tomas Bata University (a 1999 English translation of the first edition by Josef Hassmann and Myron Tribus is in private circulation).

Sarasohn, Homer M. and Charles B. Protzman (1948, 1998), *The Fundamentals of Industrial Management*, electronic edition edited by N.I. Fisher, available at http://deming-network.org/giants_sarasohn.htm.

Sutcliff, Michael R. and Michael Donnellan (2006), *CFO Insights: Delivering High Performance*, Chichester: John Wiley and Sons.

Tinsley, C. H., R. L. Dillon and P. M. Madsen (2011), "How to avoid catastrophe," *Harvard Business Review*, 89 (4) (April), 90–7.

Ulrich, Dave and Norm Smallwood (2003), *Why the Bottom Line Isn't! How to Build Value Through People and Organizations*, Hoboken, N.J.: John Wiley and Sons.

Vine, F. J. (1968), "Magnetic anomalies associated with mid-ocean ridges," pages 73–89 in *The History of the Earth's Crust: A Symposium*, edited by Robert A Phinney, Princeton, N.J.: Princeton University Press.

Vogel, Norbert J. (2008), *Performance Excellence Guide for Regional Natural Resource Management Organizations*, second edition, available at www.amlrnrm.sa.gov.au/Portals/2/reports/Performance%20Excellence%20Guide%20for%20Regional%20Natural%20Resource%20~%202nd%20Edition%20February%202008.pdf.

Index